# Full Spectrum Supervision

*"Who you are, is how you supervise"*

*Dedication*

*This book is dedicated to our students at the
Coaching Supervision Academy (CSA). For seven
years they have engaged wholeheartedly with their
supervision training, learned with us, laughed
with us and taught us so much.*

# Full Spectrum Supervision

### "Who you are, is how you supervise"

Edited by
## Edna Murdoch and Jackie Arnold

Panoma
PRESS

# *Preface*

IN THIS book we have brought together seven authors who have contributed significantly  to the emerging profession of coaching supervision. Each of them has trained and qualified as a coach supervisor, in addition to their considerable experience in this area and their other professional qualifications.

Each chapter focuses on a specific element of supervision and its relationship to the Full Spectrum Model (FSM) (see the Introduction).

Case studies, tips and exercises clearly present each element of supervision in practical terms. The variety of methodologies underlines the diversity of perspectives and supervision approaches included in the chapters.

We hope you enjoy the journey of discovery.

**Edna Murdoch** and **Jackie Arnold**

# Full Spectrum Supervision

*"Who you are, is how you supervise"*

First published in 2013 by
Panoma Press Ltd
48 St Vincent Drive, St Albans, Herts, AL1 5SJ UK
info@panomapress.com
www.panomapress.com

Cover design by Michael Inns
Artwork by Karen Gladwell
Jackie Arnold Portrait by Stephen Cotterell Photography

Printed on acid-free paper from managed forests. This book is printed on demand to fulfill orders, so no copies will be remaindered or pulped.

ISBN 978-1-908746-99-3

# Contents

# Contributors

**EDNA MURDOCH** – director, Coaching Supervision Academy

Edna provides supervision internationally for major coaching companies, business groups, independent executive coaches, human resources (HR) personnel and other professionals. She also runs supervision groups for coaches, both face to face and on the telephone, and has established a successful training program for in-house coaches who wish to establish peer supervision groups. Conference presentations on supervision include those for Oxford Brookes University, the European Mentoring and Coaching Council (EMCC) and the International Coach Federation (ICF).

Edna has worked with individuals and groups for more than 30 years. She is an educator, a coach, a coach supervisor, a writer and a presenter. In these contexts, Edna has worked with a wide range of individuals and groups. Companies and organizations that she has worked for include the Henley Business School (the University of Reading, UK), Hanover Foundations (charity, London, UK), Sussex Police (UK), Channel 4, Microsoft Corporation, NTL Incorporated, PSNI, and the Pellin (Gestalt) Institute (Italy).

She has trained extensively in coaching, group dynamics and psychotherapy, as well as in constellations work with Judith Hemmings. In 2001 Edna pioneered one of the first supervision services for coaches in the UK. She then founded CSA and became a director of the Coaching Supervision Academy. Edna co-designed the CSA's diploma in coaching supervision and has trained more than 200 executive coaches in supervision.

Edna may be found at
**www.coachingsupervisionacademy.com**
and may be contacted at **edna@csa.uk.net**

# ALISON HODGE

Graduating in Australia, Alison started her commercial career in the UK in 1973 in the field of business magazine publishing. Her roles included sales management, publishing and head of training, managing teams of up to 60 people.

In May 1985 Alison set up her own sales and management training consultancy. Since completing her MSc in change agent skills and strategies in 2000, she now focuses primarily on coaching supervision alongside team facilitation and coaching.

Alison's supervision is based on co-creating collaborative learning relationships that support her clients' personal and professional development as either internal or external coaches, to insure that they deliver the best possible service to their clients.

Coupled with excellent communication skills, she uses creative interventions to address individual, group and organizational change issues. Her professional practice is underpinned by the Ethical Codes from the EMCC and the Association for Professional Executive Coaching and Supervision (APECS). She brings a personal empathy to her client relationships, with academic appreciation and understanding of change processes. Alison is valued for her passionate enthusiasm and for her belief in people's ability to succeed and grow.

She has been practicing Taiji (a meditation system, health practice and martial art) for 17 years, which she believes helps to keep her grounded and mindful in her work and relationships.

Alison is reading for her professional doctorate in coaching supervision at Middlesex University in North London.

Alison may be found at **www.alisonhodge.com** and may be contacted at **Alison@alisonhodge.com**

## JACKIE ARNOLD

Jackie has been an executive coach and coach trainer since 1998. One of the founding board members of the UK ICF from 2001 until 2004, she holds an ICF-recognized coaching qualification, is an NLP practitioner and clean language facilitator and holds the CSA diploma in coaching supervision. She is a board member of the Association of Coaching Supervisors (AOCS).

Jackie has a real passion for developing effective leaders at all levels in both the public sector and the private. This has been mainly through integrated coaching programs, one-to-one coaching and supervision.

As well as supporting senior executives, she has delivered the Institute of Leadership & Management (ILM) and Chartered Management Institute (CMI) qualifications to more than 200 managers and leaders including those in the National Health Service (NHS), Shell B2B, The Co-Operative Bank plc (UK), Kent county council, and Die Klubschule Migros (Switzerland). High-quality facilitation with clean language, NLP and skilled coaching interventions insures that leaders are working to their full potential. She is also currently working for Airbus as a leadership coach in Filton, Bristol.

Jackie is a regular conference speaker and an author of five books, the most recent being *Coaching Skills for Leaders in the Workplace: How to develop, motivate and get the best from your staff* (published by How To Books) and *Get That Job with NLP* (published by Hodder Education). She has been commissioned to write a book on coaching supervision in the workplace to be published by Crown House and due out in autumn 2013.

Jackie may be found at **www.coach4executives.com** and **www.associationofcoachingsupervisors.com** and may be contacted at **jackie@coach4executives.com**

## SAMUEL P. MAGILL SR.

Sam Magill (MCC) is a coach of coaches. As one of a small number of executive coaches in the US who has specifically studied and been certified in the oversight of other coaches, he offers high-level insight and skills in the development of people who want to become coaches. His executive clients benefit from this special work because Sam is constantly learning about the real factors that support good coaching.

With 30 years of experience in organization and leadership development, Sam brings a rich understanding of issues faced by leaders in settings as diverse as health clinics and high-tech research labs. He helps his clients interpret their experiences and create new responses to complex challenges. Sam continues to learn about coaching and leadership by teaching on master's degree programs and on top-ranked coaching programs. Sam will become president of the Puget Sound Coaches Association (PSCA), a local chapter of the ICF.

A Master Certified Coach (ICF), Sam has operated his own coaching practice since 1996. He began his coaching and consulting practice as an internal practitioner and manager at The Boeing Company in 1988. He holds a master's in business administration from California State University, East Bay, 1977, and is a graduate of the Hudson Institute of Santa Barbara where he also taught coaching from 2002 to 2008. Sam completed the accredited diploma program at the Coaching Supervision Academy, London, England, in 2010.

His broad understanding of how people work is enhanced through his work as a poet and as a photographer. In 2006, he published his first book of poetry, *Fully Human*.

Sam may be found at **www.sammagill.com** and may be contacted at **sam@sammagill.com**

## ELAINE PATTERSON

Elaine is an international executive coach and learning facilitator. Elaine is an accredited EMCC master practitioner coach mentor and she qualified as an accredited coach supervisor with the Coaching Supervision Academy in 2009.

Elaine has held a range of leading-edge director roles in the NHS, in the civil service and in the voluntary sector and has coached and supervised leaders extensively across the public, private and voluntary sectors.

Elaine brings her natural compassion, courage and humanity to her executive coaching and coaching supervision practice. She draws her inspiration from literature, art, photography and film.

Elaine is also a published writer in the coaching professional press. Publications include *Presence in Coaching Supervision* for the Association for Coaching, *Supervision in Coaching: Supervision, ethics, CPD and the law, Transformational Learning* and *Learning through the Art of Conversation* with Liz Buckle. She contributed to *Coaching and Mentoring: Practical conversations to support learning* with Eric Parsloe and Mel Ledham.

Elaine is currently studying for an MA in reflective learning at Middlesex University and has established a new executive coaching, coaching supervision and learning facilitation practice called the LftF practice with co-founders Liz Buckle and Maren Donata Urschel (visit **www.lftf.eu.**).

Elaine can be contacted at **Elaine.patterson@lftf.eu**

# IAN MACKENZIE

**Ian's passion is helping people to develop their own insights – that is, to understand themselves and others, including motivations – and to use that information positively and effectively.**

Ian has been working with these themes for more than 30 years. In one stream Ian has developed effective leaders at all levels for a wide range of organizations, through workshops, integrated training programs and one-to-one coaching and mentoring.

In 1998, having worked for American Express (AmEx) and a Brighton consultancy, he co-founded Learning Navigators – a network that pioneered innovative, integrated work-based leadership programs in organizations as diverse as the Department for Education (Dfe) and Credit Suisse (headquartered in Zürich, Switzerland).

The other stream is his continuous exploration of insight and how it develops – leading him to learn, practice and teach meditation, study at the Centre for Transpersonal Psychology (CTP) (based in the UK) and teach meditation.

Working as a coach, a supervisor and a tutor with the Coaching Supervision Academy, Ian is increasingly bringing these two streams together. He is exploring the relationships between mindfulness, presence and insight and how these are the foundations for excellence in coaching, mentoring and leadership.

Ian recently co-founded The Presence Partnership and is currently planning a series of workshops exploring meditation and presence for coaches and supervisors.

Ian may be found at **www.ian-mackenzie.co.uk** and may be contacted at **ian@ian-mackenzie.co.uk**

# KATE LANZ

Over the past 14 years Kate has built a reputation as a first-class executive coach. She combines 12 years of senior level corporate experience with psychological training to help business leaders achieve lasting behavioral change. Kate specializes in coaching individual executives at the higher levels of the organization. Kate is a qualified supervisor (CSA) and supervises other senior practitioners in both individual and group settings. She also coaches and supervises at INSEAD, the global business school.

Kate's corporate career has centered on multinational organizations, notably Diageo. She successfully held international roles in marketing, sales and general management. In the course of her extensive global business experience, Kate has lived and worked in six countries. Kate has a degree in French and German, a postgraduate degree in Marketing and an MBA and a BSc in Psychology.

Kate has coached leaders across a broad spectrum of sectors from Board Directors of large multinationals to startups. Her clients include Pfizer, Smith & Nephew, IKEA, Ernst & Young, Deutsche Bank AG, Disney, Diageo, EDF Energy, the Co-operative Group, AXA Insurance and several large, not-for-profit organizations. Kate divides her time between coaching, supervising and writing on both coaching and coaching supervision.

Kate may be found at **www.lanzexecutivecoaching.co.uk** and can be contacted at **kate@lanzexecutivecoaching.co.uk**

## KARYN PRENTICE

Karyn is an assistant director at the CSA, working on their UK, French and US coaching supervision diploma and continuing professional development (CPD) programs. Karyn has been coaching for more than 15 years (CPID, OCM) and an accredited coach supervisor (CSA) since 2008. She coaches individuals at the most senior level of organizational life, with supervisees internationally and groups in the UK. She is an external coach for PWC. Karyn is passionate about supervision as a way to enable and resource coaches to be the very best they can be. Karyn is also a UK Council for Psychotherapy (UKCP) accredited transpersonal psychotherapist.

Fletcher-Prentice & Associates has been established since 1995. Working across a broad landscape of public, corporate and private sectors and more than 40 institutions of further and higher education, Karyn designs and facilitates leadership programs and team and group learning events for building relationships and increasing effective communication. Karyn is currently teaching two master's level programs on reflective practice and on advanced coaching skills for Teeside University's business clients.

Karyn presents at a variety of conferences and writes for a number of journals. She divides her time between France and the UK.

Karyn may be found at **www.fletcherprentice.com** and may be contacted at **karyn@csa.uk.net**

# *Foreword*
## by Lise Lewis, EMCC president

WHAT A privilege to write this foreword for CSA, pioneers in designing and offering coach supervision training and instrumental in providing leading-edge materials for the maturing coaching industry. CSA are also among the first group of organizations to be awarded the European Supervision Quality Award (ESQA) for supervision training courses. This award was recently launched by the European Mentoring and Coaching Council (EMCC), which is the only professional body at this time offering a quality award specifically for supervision training.

I first met Edna Murdoch and Miriam Orriss of CSA at an EMCC conference held at Ashridge, Hertfordshire, UK in 2007. I was immediately struck by their warmth of greeting toward a new acquaintance quickly followed by their obvious passion for professionalism in supervision. Their skill, expertise and topic knowledge was clearly evident in this first exchange and it's no surprise that their supervision training continues to attract those seeking a quality experience.

CSA has recognized and contributed to valuing the intrinsic worth of supervision for individuals. For organizations the merit of engaging with and sourcing supervision for both their internal and external coaches is seen as fundamental to securing a good return on what can be a high investment development option. The expectation is that supervision will be instrumental in supporting the building and application of coaching skills and knowledge capability to improve and maximize clients' performance. The ripple effect of this growing competence in clients permeates the organization through their interaction with others. The long-term forecast is creating a coaching culture ultimately improving overall organizational performance.

Applying good practice from the widely accepted norm of supervision in the people professions has presented a bridge for offering a similar approach in the younger industry of coaching. However, as coaching has developed as a discipline so has the need for supervision to be more specifically related to coaching. Drawing on the history and evolution of supervision in other professions, Hawkins and Smith (2006) define three main functions of effective coaching supervision as

1. qualitative (providing quality control in working ethically with people)
2. developmental (skills, understanding and capabilities) and
3. resourcing (providing emotional support).

In addition to these three main functions, coaches may not have the expertise to "identify mental-health issues impinging on the boundaries of coaching" and they may be "less prepared to identify the effect of their personal process on their work because they are not required ... to undertake ... counselling or other personal development" (Bachkirova, Jackson and Clutterbuck, 2011).

From a macro perspective, as an unregulated industry the future of coaching being acknowledged as a powerful development intervention will depend on those involved demonstrating professional practice. Resulting from the creation of the Global Coaching and Mentoring Alliance (GCMA) created at the EMCC conference in Bilbao 2012 between the Association for Coaching (AC), the EMCC and the ICF, these professional bodies will be working with an international remit for professionalizing the industry and to demonstrate self-regulation. The Professional Charter for Coaching and Mentoring is already lodged in the European Union (EU) in support of this. This Charter sets out indicators and expectations for professional practice from their members, including regular engagement in coach supervision.

The CSA is responding to all of these challenges by producing this evidence- and practice-based publication, taking supervision to another level appropriate for coaching now and in the future. The text offers a richness of content from a diverse range of specialists who are experts in their field. For a supervisor wishing to deepen and broaden his or her practice or for coaches/mentors wanting to access a text before, during and following training this is a superior resource based on the Full Spectrum Model.

## www.coachingsupervisionacademy.com/ourapproach/ fullspectrummodel

The Full Spectrum Model is an eclectic mix of theoretical approaches synergistically combined into a holistic systemic framework. Color-coded components represent different reference points for ease of access for the reader. This is a fully integrated model offering a significant range of tools, techniques and models drawn from various disciplines. A flavor of what to expect is a theoretical underpinning applied to practice from adult learning theory, systemics, mindfulness, relational psychology, neuroscience, quantum physics, advanced dialog process, spirituality and more, combined to enhance supervision relationships.

As coaches are increasingly asked about quality managing their practice including arrangements for supervision, this is likely to be paralleled by a growth in demand for well-trained professional supervisors. This text has to be included as core reading for anyone serious about supervision and I'm sure will be valued as essential reading for all those who have any involvement in supervision. You will be invited to sample materials available in CSA trainings as an insight into what is available experientially.

**Lise Lewis**
**President, European Mentoring and Coaching Council**

## REFERENCES
**Bachkirova, T, Jackson, P and Clutterbuck, D (2011)** *Coaching and Mentoring Supervision*, Berkshire, UK: Open University Press.

**Hawkins, P and Smith, N (2006)** *Coaching, Mentoring and Organizational Consultancy: Supervision and development,* Maidenhead, UK: Open University Press.

# Introduction
# *Overview of coaching supervision*

- Edna Murdoch

## Vision for the book

I WAS fortunate that shortly after qualifying as a psychotherapist many years ago, I found a supervisor who would walk with me, get me thinking about my work in new ways and who would support me when I came to the edge of my competence or when I felt overwhelmed. The main ingredients of our conversations stand out now – engagement and joy. It was clear that we both enjoyed the fortnightly delving into the work, my struggles with aspects of that work and the celebrations that followed successful sessions or increased competence. Joy is sometimes overlooked – it is a key ingredient of learning and this was truly a learning partnership. Other supervisors followed and I became fascinated by the range and depth of the conversations that supervision offered. Eventually I trained as a supervisor and worked with senior managers, business leaders and psychotherapists for many years.

When I began to coach (in 1999), I fully expected to continue this level of professional development and support; however, at that time there was little supervision for coaches and it was some time before I found good coaching supervision for the new work. It was not long before I too began to supervise coaches and to learn – sometimes through difficult feedback – what kind of supervision served the coaching profession. Others in the field were also developing a supervision fit for purpose and it is marvelous to see how quickly coaching supervision has become the main form of CPD for many coaches – and how much care and original thinking has gone into creating the multidisciplinary practice that we recognize today as coaching supervision. The CSA was established to meet the vacuum we had identified and it has developed in to a worldwide community of CSA-qualified supervisors whose inspired learning journeys have helped us to develop the ideas in this book.

The practice of supervision is still evolving and coaches across the world are now training in coaching supervision. The ICF recently accepted the role of the coach supervisor and in an important statement said:

Coaching Supervision is the interaction that occurs when a coach periodically brings his or her coaching work experiences to a coaching supervisor in order to engage in reflective dialogue and collaborative learning for the development and benefit of the coach and his or her clients ...

Coaching Supervision is distinct from Mentor Coaching for Credentialing. Mentor Coaching focuses on the development of coaching skills mainly in the context of initial development. Coaching Supervision offers the coach a richer and broader opportunity for support and development. In Coaching Supervision, the coach is invited to focus much more on what is going on in their process and where the personal may be intruding on the professional.

**ICF Webarchive, 2012**

## Who is this book for?

This book is for anyone who is interested in the practice of supervision. It is for coaches, coach supervisors, mentors and those who employ coaches and supervisors. However, much of what is written in these chapters is relevant to any session in which one professional is in conversation with another with the express purpose of creating a reflective space for learning, support and development. It is for anyone who wants to know what happens in supervision and how it brings a rigorous, ongoing developmental process to professionals at all levels.

Although the key focus of these chapters is on the work with coaches, the material also relates to supervision with therapists, social workers, managers and public sector workers. Supervisory process is used in many other contexts too: in boardrooms, with HR professionals, business leaders, educators and health professionals. We hope that practitioners in many contexts will benefit from reading about the practice of supervision. The words 'coach', 'practitioner' and 'professional' are used interchangeably throughout the book.

The book takes the reader into the heart of the practice of supervision – its methods, models and magic. Using case study focus and the Full Spectrum Model of supervision as a guide – see below – the book brings supervision to life and shows how this transformative professional conversation supports and develops anyone who works closely with other practitioners. Readers will discover how the practical and profound inquiry of supervision frees up practitioners to work more intelligently – with humanity and skillfulness. Supervision offers a unique space – a space in which practitioners reflect on their work and become more effective in taking care of their organizations, their teams, their clients and themselves. The book will illustrate how supervision draws on adult learning theory, systems theory, the art of reflection, mindfulness, relational psychology, neuroscience, advanced dialog process, psychology, spirituality and more. These provide a rich resource for the reflective practice known as supervision; they bring depth and richness to classic supervision maps and models.

Recent publications on supervision and coaching supervision have highlighted key elements of supervisory inquiry and explored some of the tools that are used by supervisors. We will add to that list, but we will also focus on aspects of a supervisor's work that draw on skills such as mindfulness – a powerful and practical methodology, embodied presence, transpersonal psychology and heart-to-heart work, now underpinned by discoveries in contemporary science. This book will also demonstrate some of the domains that support inquiry in supervision:

▼ *clean language*

▼ *metaphor and imagery*

▼ *use of visualization*

▼ *full body presence*

▼ *working with the unconscious and with parallel process*

▼ *collective consciousness*

▼ *field theory*

▼ *relational skills*

▼ *quantum physics*

▼ *systems theory*

▼ *reflection in action*

▼ *the nature of skilled accompaniment.*

All of this supports the important supervisory responsibility of ensuring that practice is ethical and that professional standards are upheld. *The buck stops with the supervisor* and it is his or her responsibility to insure that professionals know how to meet their contractual obligations. A skilled supervisor can do this without becoming oppressive, through engaging the coach's interest and commitment to best practice and by imaginatively drawing the coach into inquiring into his or her own skills and capacities.

## What is coaching supervision? What does it do?

In chapter one, Alison Hodge usefully defines supervision as:

A co-created learning relationship that supports the supervisee in his or her development, both personally and professionally, and seeks to support him or her in providing best practice to his or her client. Through the process of reflecting on his or her work in supervision, the supervisee can review and develop his or her practice and re-energize him or herself. It offers a forum to attend to his or her emotional and professional wellbeing and growth. Through the relationship and dialog in this alliance, coaches can receive feedback, broaden their perspectives, generate new ideas and maintain standards of effective practice.

Supervision involves working skillfully with generating new ideas, honing interventions, understanding relational dynamics and reducing fear and shame. It increases generative dialog, growth, commitment, competence, engagement, new ideas and heart work. The specifics of this work insure that practitioners have support with:

▼ *clear contracting – including multiparty contracting*

▼ *establishing good boundaries*

▼ *enhancing reflectivity – working with content and process*

▼ *attending to the coach's personal development*

▼ *creating the working alliance*

▼ *deepening practitioner presence*

▼ *building the internal supervisor*

▼ *gaining new perspectives*

▼ *developing meta-skills*

▼ *increasing interventions and tools*

▼ *learning about relational psychology*

▼ *working with parallel process*

▼ *working within systems*

▼ *ensuring professional standards*

▼ *increasing professional range and competence.*

In this conversation, the full range of the self is engaged – thinking, feeling and body. Supervision is potentially a transformative conversation. It invites both parties to move into the unknown with confidence, in order to learn together. It is a conversational space full of possibilities – and of risk. At its best, it encourages profound attention and full body/mind/spirit presence and insures deep learning. At its worst, it can be practiced as a tick-box activity, policing in its intentions, and, in this mode, it can easily narrow the capacity for learning and development. Good supervision enables supervisees to slow down thinking and increase observation, to notice the whole field in which their work is unfolding. It also enables them to be excited by the emergence of new ideas and new perspectives. It returns the practitioner to his or her work, resourced, empowered and fully engaged in self-observation and in his or her own learning.

In his early work, Otto Sharmer outlines some of the key features of successful conversation: co-sensing, co-creating, co-evolving and seeing from the emerging whole. He suggests a quality of presence in conversation where you "attend with your mind wide open". This perfectly describes the nature of supervisory exploration and this quality of attention is amply illustrated in the chapters of this book. These chapters show how supervision lifts the coach from the minutiae of a coach's individual sessions to the open spaces where ideas can flow and new learning can emerge. Here a coach can experience a significant increase in professional capacity. The knock-on benefit is that, as professionals develop through supervision, so do the systems in which they are working.

The robustness of supervisory exploration and its key role in coaches' learning and development are what give protection to coaches and to commissioning agents. It insures that internal and external coaches are not only practicing in ways that meet their contractual obligations, but are also growing, not stagnating. The field conditions that govern this level of conversational activity mean that where the individual coach and the system meet, there is an exchange of information. In this way, organizations absorb the coach's learning, either directly as feedback or indirectly as the result of informational exchange in the energetic field.

## "Who you are is how you supervise"

One of the catchphrases associated with CSA is: "Who you are is how you coach." This emerged many years ago in conversation with my colleague, Aboodi Shabi, with whom I have had many vigorous conversations about how we show up in a relational profession. I can now also say: "Who you are is how you supervise." My experience is that operating alongside all of our professional trainings, our thinking, tools and models, is the personhood of the practitioner – our humanity matters, as does our maturity, our open-heartedness and our generosity of spirit. All of these are of crucial importance in the learning environment of supervision; they serve to build a quality of relationship that enables transparency from both parties and thus has the potential to create a real shift in the supervisee's practice.

Supervision is essentially a conversation about other conversations – conversations between buyers, managers, sponsors, coaches, coachees, board members and HR personnel. There are professional and business conversations, contractual conversations, financial ones, fruitful and difficult ones, truthful and tricky conversations – all the usual conversational activity that is part of the fabric of every large or small organization. The challenge to every professional is: Who am I in this conversation? And to every supervisor: How do I enter this field of conversation so that my supervisee becomes better at what he or she does?

## Field conditions

These conversations are further affected by what Ervin Lazlo, philosopher and Nobel Prize winner, describes as "the living field of energy", out of which everything arises and within which we live. In the world of quantum physics, we are all connected, all the time and in every place.

At this level we discover that ALL matter is energy – the desk, the car, you, and me. There is no solid boundary between matter and non matter, and both are made up of the same thing – energy, or quantum particles.

(Miriam Orriss, 2006; see 'Resources' at
**www.coachingsupervisionacademy.com**)

Lazlo says that the Field is one vast interconnected field of information. So, when we begin to work with an individual or a group, we enter into and increase the energetic space that contains our creativity, thinking and intentions for the work. This begins to happen from the moment that a potential employer or supervisee contacts a supervisor and it continues as we converse and contract for the work. Knowing how to utilize this in supervisory conversation greatly increases the impact of that conversation.

## Full Spectrum Model of supervision

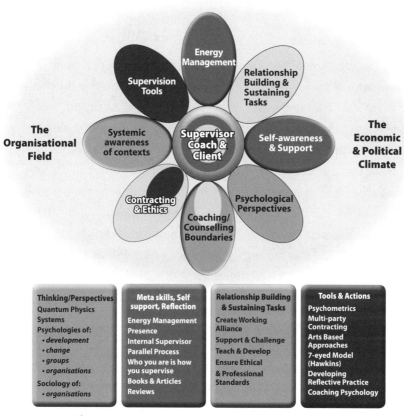

© COACHING SUPERVISION ACADEMY **www.coachingsupervisionacademy.com**

*For a colour version of the Full Spectrum Model, go to :*

**www.coachingsupervisionacademy.com/ourapproach/
fullspectrummodel**

The Full Spectrum Model (FSM) of supervision has been developed by the Coaching Supervision Academy to show the multilayered activity that is supervision – in any professional context. As we know, maps and models are not the practice, but they can highlight processes and guide our practice. This model can be used by the supervisor as a means to inform his or her practice and also as means of exploring with a supervisee the full range of the conversation he or she can have in supervision. It also points to tools and techniques that enhance practice both practically and creatively.

The creation of the Full Spectrum Model of supervision was in part a response to the awareness of "Who you are is how you coach". My colleagues, Miriam Orriss and Fiona Adamson, and I, wanted the model to highlight the centrality of the relationships in supervision – those between the supervisor and the supervisee and those that operate in the wider system and have impact all the way into the supervision session. This relational field, as it is sometimes known, has significant influence on each professional conversation. All the perspectives on the Full Spectrum Model touch the core relational circle, because they influence or are influenced by, the supervisor–supervisee relationship.

The FSM offers supervisors a powerful range of professional development tools and insights, which span 20th- and 21st-century knowledge, and it combines traditional and contemporary methods and models. It utilizes knowledge gained through attending to classic models of supervision as well as through attending to the body, mind and spirit. This holistic and integrative model also rests on ancient wisdoms, a sense of our shared humanity and what it is to be human in practice and in the workplace. This perspective brings lively, energetic and radical understanding to all the relationships that are at the center of coaching and establishing coaching contracts. The model amplifies the need for supervisors

# I Coaching supervision - an ethical angle

- Alison Hodge

## Abstract

IN THIS chapter we establish the ethical context in which we work as supervisors to support coaches to provide the best possible service to their clients – both individually and corporately. As coaching establishes itself as a "profession" (Spence, 2007: 261; Bennett, 2006; Lane cited in Bachkirova, 2011), many of us continue to explore the role and practice of supervision in supporting coaches to meet the demands of this highly complex practice. While there are numerous examples of Ethical Codes available in the field of coaching, ethical dilemmas may still arise for the coach. Often these are the issues that the coach brings to us in supervision, and our mutual task of how to address these is not always straightforward. When the coach creates a coaching contract between him or herself, the client and the sponsoring organization we find the bedrock that may pre-empt many of the ethical issues that reportedly occur. Here we explore the professional, practical and psychological dimensions of the coaching contract and how these support everyone involved.

## Introduction

As coaching continues to blossom in the UK, there is a groundswell of interest in how we become more professional. Conversations about "professionalism" and "ethical practice" are gathering momentum (Lane, Stelter and Rostron, 2010). We are seeing significant efforts dedicated to the process of coach accreditation and, as part of this, coaching associations are seeking to validate the coach's awareness and understanding of a professional Ethical Code of Conduct and to seek evidence of this in his or her practice (Lane, 2011).

I have been working as a coaching supervisor for the past 12 years. My coach-clients practice in a wide range of contexts including the corporate and public sectors as well as in education. Through my involvement in facilitating ethical awareness workshops for both external and internal coaches throughout the UK and Europe, I am constantly reminded that many coaches face diverse incidents on a daily basis during coaching assignments, which may or may not be described as "ethical dilemmas" and to which there is not always an obvious or easy answer or solution.

In this chapter, we look at the types of incidents that arise during coaching assignments across a wide range of coaching contexts, why these may occur, the role of the different stakeholders in contracting to create robust, ethical coaching alliances and the role of supervision in supporting coaches in managing themselves and these issues both professionally and ethically. Here too we notice how this ethical dimension flows through all of the other elements of the Full Spectrum Model.

Before we enter this discussion, and given the diverse participants who may be involved in the coaching and therefore supervision relationships, I have created a glossary to describe frequently used terms as well as the different and potential stakeholders.

## Glossary

**'Ethics'** – "a system of moral principles that affect the way in which people make decisions and lead their lives" (Townsend cited in Passmore, 2011).

**'Ethical practice'** – "The coach/mentor will acknowledge the dignity of all humanity. They will conduct themselves in a way which respects diversity and promotes equal opportunities. It is the primary responsibility of the coach/mentor to provide the best possible service to the client and to act in such a way as to cause no harm to any client or sponsor. The coach/mentor is committed to functioning from a position of dignity, autonomy and personal responsibility" (EMCC UK, 2010).

**'The client'** – the participant/receiver of coaching in the coaching assignment.

**'Line manager'** – the person to whom the client reports in an organizational context.

**'Sponsor'** – the budget holder and/or champion of the coaching initiative, particularly in an organizational context.

**'The coach' (supervisee)** – 'External coach' – an independent professional practitioner who provides the actual coaching service. He or she may operate through his or her own business or he or she may be retained as an associate of a larger coaching consultancy.

**'Internal coach'** – an employee in the client organization who provides coaching services to other employees on either a full- or part-time basis.

**'Consultancy principal'** – head of the coaching consultancy providing coaches to the client organization.

**'Multipartite agreements'** – where all parties in the coaching assignment are both implicitly and explicitly involved, i.e. client, line manager, sponsor and coach.

**'Stakeholder'** – any person connected with the client who will benefit from the outcomes.

**'The coaching supervisor'** – a qualified practitioner who provides coaching supervision to either internal or external coaches.

**'Full Spectrum Model'** – offers a powerful range of professional development tools and insights that ... combine traditional and contemporary methods and models applied in supervision. Uniquely, FSM has at its core, Coaching Presence and the awareness of the total Field in which coaching operates across mind, body and spirit (coachingsupervisionacademy.com/our-approach/full-spectrum-model).

**'Coaching supervision'**– "A co-created learning relationship that supports the supervisee in his or her development, both personally and professionally, and seeks to support him or her in providing best practice to his or her client. Through the process of reflecting on his or her work in supervision, the supervisee can review and develop his or her practice and re-energize themselves. It offers a forum to attend to his or her emotional and professional wellbeing and growth. Through the relationship and dialog in this alliance, coaches can receive feedback, broaden their perspectives, generate new ideas and maintain standards of effective practice" (Alison Hodge, 2011).

## Ethical issues that arise in supervision

In 2008, the EMCC conducted some research among its members that established that coaches would welcome a workshop that discussed and addressed ethical issues. These sessions have now been running regularly throughout the UK and the examples discussed here are representative of the incidents that arise for coaches and their clients and that as supervisors we are likely to explore with coaches during our supervision together.

Subsequent research in 2009 (St John-Brooks, 2010) aimed to identify the ethical dilemmas experienced by internal coaches in the UK and that are not confined solely to internal coaches.

In the figure below, we see some of the domains where issues arise during coaching assignments, for both external and internal coaches.

## Domains where issues arise during coaching assignments

▼ Line managers in the client organization want information or feedback about the client and/or information or feedback regarding the progress of the coaching.

▼ Line managers want separate conversations with the coach about the purpose of the coaching and that are not shared with the client – the manager's agenda.

▼ There is conflict of roles and interests where the coach (be they internal or external) holds more than one role within the organization, e.g. coach, facilitator, leadership and development trainer, human resources business adviser and/or OD consultant.

▼ The client wants to explore issues that involve someone else in the organization that the coach knows well, or works with, and/or is sponsored by.

▼ The client describes inappropriate comments or behavior by a third party in the organization and the coach is not able to act on this under the terms of his or her confidentiality agreement, e.g. harassment or bullying.

▼ The client has significant personal issues that have an effect on his or her performance that they share with the coach but do not want anyone else to know.

▼ The coach is privy to knowledge about the client/client's future (for example, regarding restructuring or redundancy) that he or she does not know and the coach can't tell him or her.

▼ *The coach gathers information about a team or the organization that could be of benefit but is unable to share this information within the boundary of confidentiality.*

▼ *The client attempts to use sessions to further his or her own agenda by influencing the coach, inviting collusion by the coach.*

▼ *The client wants to discuss leaving the organization, which their line manager may not be aware of.*

▼ *There are boundary issues between the coach and the client and/or between the supervisor and the coach.*

## Emergence of ethical issues in coaching

It's not always immediately clear why these issues arise. Here we look at some of the contributing factors.

It may not be easy to include the line manager in the original dialog when the coaching agreement is established. Sometimes the client goes directly to human resources to set up the coaching, or even sources a coach directly for him or herself through referral, so the line manager is not privy to or included in the process. This may be for a variety of reasons including the fact that the client may have issues with his or her line manager that he or she wishes to address in the coaching conversation.

Inevitably it is possible therefore that the line manager may feel 'left out of the loop' and it is probably not surprising that he or she wants to know what outcomes he or she may expect from the coaching, especially when it may be coming from his or her budget. So how does the coach respond to his or her curiosity and interest?

Equally, the line manager may have concerns with an employee's performance, and without necessarily being aware of the part he or she could or should play in this relationship, he or she may lack the know-how or the skills to address these and consequently seek coaching as the solution. In fact, it may become apparent that the line manager needs coaching – so what does the coach do with this 'diagnosis'?

Many coaches may hold more than one role with their organizational client, e.g. as internal coach he or she is also a line manager, or as external coach he or she is also facilitating team development or leadership programs. Here he or she is engaged with a number of employees and he or she is in multiple relationships. The question then arises as to how he or she holds his or her boundaries between the different tasks, containing the confidential content for any one client, avoiding conflicts of interest and at the same time gathering valuable insights that would serve the organization well if only they could be shared. So what are the boundaries of confidentiality in these instances and how does the coach manage these? And how may he or she set up a process that enables him or her to share his or her insights without compromising the confidentiality of the coaching conversation?

Then there are the personal incidents and events that the client shares with the coach that may be affecting his or her performance and wellbeing. So, what does the coach do, aside from recommending or referring for different sources of support, e.g. counseling or medical, when a client shows up distressed, disturbed or unwell and he or she does not wish to involve anyone else in the organization?

Sometimes the client wants to leave his or her organization or indeed he or she may be involved in some form of employment tribunal, and he or she finds great value in being able to explore these issues with an external/objective trusted confidant, i.e. his or her coach. So, how does the coach respond in these circumstances?

Is this on the agenda? What are the legal implications? To whom is the coach responsible or accountable?

The following case study provides an example of a dilemma that a coach brought to me in supervision.

### An example of a dilemma brought to supervision

Mavis is an experienced executive coach who comes to supervision with me monthly. On one occasion she arrives and wants to discuss the work she is doing with her client, Richard. She has had four sessions with Richard and he doesn't appear to be making any changes or adopting any of the actions agreed during the coaching sessions. Mavis is wondering what is wrong, questioning whether it is her coaching, something with Richard or there is something else going on.

In our discussions, Mavis realizes that she has not actually asked Richard directly about this until now, and agrees to do so when they next meet. When she returns to her next coaching session and raises the subject, Richard admits to her that his marriage is breaking up and he is about to be thrown out of the marital home – he is clearly very distressed, and he may be even be depressed. At this point, therefore, Mavis puts the 'Pause Button' on the coaching, and discusses with Richard what support he most needs at this time and whether the coaching he is receiving is appropriate or useful.

In this instance, Richard agreed that he would be better supported with some counseling to help him sort out the next best steps for him at home, before trying to meet work-based goals for which he had no energy or concentration. He also agreed to speak to HR (which he had not done before this point) so they could support him internally.

Mavis' dilemma lay in being uncertain in whether or how best to raise Richard's lack of action between coaching sessions. Once she raised the issue and established the cause, she was able to re-contract, agreeing that the help Richard needed was outside of her coaching agreement and skills set.

Here now are some further live examples of actual incidents that the coach may have to deal with during any coaching assignment and which coaches frequently bring to supervision to explore and resolve.

### Try this now

How would you respond to these incidents **(1) as the supervisor and (2) as the coach?**

As there may be no single 'right' solution to the following, consider what stance you may take with each of the following incidents described by your supervisee. What would inform your response as the supervisor and how may you help your coach explore these issues?

▼ *A client arrives at coaching sessions smelling of alcohol.*

▼ *The client has agreed performance goals to help her be promoted. Her line manager has told the coach separately that her employment is in jeopardy.*

▼ The client hints that he would like more than a professional relationship with the coach.

▼ The coach is attracted to the client.

▼ The coach is coaching three individual members of the board. The CEO tells the coach that she is worried about one of these individuals.

▼ The client comes to a coaching session and tells the coach that he is being sexually harassed by his line manager.

▼ The client appears to be making no change after four coaching sessions.

▼ The client wants the coach's help to prepare for an industrial tribunal.

▼ The coach has had 12 coaching sessions with his client. The client is keen to extend the assignment and is willing to pay for this personally if the company will not fund the coaching.

▼ The organization's legal department wants the coach's notes of one of his clients to use in an industrial tribunal.

▼ Three individual clients tell the coach that their line manager, the coach's sponsor, is "incompetent" and is seriously threatening the success of the department. They are all thinking of leaving the company as a result.

▼ A prospective client is returning to work after a stress-related absence and her line manager has proposed that she has coaching to support her.

▼ A client asks the coach to link up on LinkedIn or Facebook.

▼ The client is a senior executive who has twice, in three months, called the day before a session to explain that he must reschedule the coaching session. The coach has a cancellation clause in the Agreement, but she is unsure whether to apply this.

▼ A client admits that he is having an extra-marital affair with a junior member of staff.

In each case, different coaches may know exactly what they would do and how they would respond, while others may not be sure, especially when an unexpected incident arises 'in the moment'. This is for a variety of reasons, some of which are based on the experience and ethical maturity of the coach (Carroll, 2009). In addition, there are complex and diverse relationships with those involved in the coaching service and within the organizational system.

So, how can the coach decide the 'best possible' and 'ethical' solutions in any given situation and, as supervisors, how can we play a significant role in helping him or her to resolve these?

| COACHES NEED | MAKING ETHICAL DECISIONS |
|---|---|
| **To be clear about their own values, be able to "bracket" these and acknowledge those which are non-negotiable (i.e. when they would walk away from an assignment).** | *Sometimes it is only when confronted by one of these incidents that the coach may become aware of their own "ethical" values. Equally, they may have to work with a client whose values are different from their own. Here the coach needs to consider the dignity and autonomy of their client without sacrificing their own integrity* |
| **To be clear about the client organization's standards, values, culture, norms and policies e.g. around discrimination, harassment, bullying and diversity.** | *An organisational briefing may not be an automatic ingredient in the initial coach-organisation discussions and the coach may not have thought to ask for this, especially when they are engaged as an associate coach.* |

| COACHES NEED | MAKING ETHICAL DECISIONS |
|---|---|
| To have clear ethical frameworks and codes of practice and they need to have shared these with their clients/sponsors. | *Many coaches profess to adhere to an Ethical Code but when asked, are unable to describe the key elements and how these inform their practice. Equally, they may not have been explicit with their clients about what informs their practice. We can help the coach in supervision to explore some of the fundamental guidelines in the Ethical Code and work out appropriate courses of action.* |
| To establish clear working agreements (i.e. contracting) at the start, with all relevant parties, e.g. sponsor, client and line manager. | *There is clear evidence that many coaching assignments fail to establish clear multi-partite agreements at the start. As we listen to an issue in supervision, we can highlight those elements that may be missing from the coaching contract.* |
| Regular supervision arrangements where they can explore these issues and dilemmas. | *More and more coaches are starting to engage in regular supervision (be this voluntary or in compliance to meet accreditation guidelines).* |
| To develop an astute "internal supervisor" to support themselves "in the moment". | *Through regular reflection on their practice and in supervision, the individual coach builds up their own capacity to support themselves "in the moment".* |

▼ *the ethical guidelines, boundaries and confidentiality*

▼ *the coaching purpose,*

▼ *the framework of the coach*

▼ *the style of the coach*

▼ *engagement of the line manager/sponsor*

▼ *evaluation and feedback processes.*

*Psychological contracting*
*– more complex and intangible – difficult to 'control'*

Here are some of the elements that may be occurring at a conscious or unconscious level within the coaching territory and that may have unexpected impacts on the coaching assignment.

**Organization** - ambiguity between declared and real purpose of the coaching, e.g. corporate culture of blame, bullying and discrimination.

**Line manager** - own fears of exposure and differing intentions from the coach.

**Client** - own agenda, past history, personal circumstances and agenda, commitment to the process/change.

**Coach** - own agenda, past history, power motives, security issues – e.g. the need for income and/or a 'clocking up' of coaching hours for accreditation.

**Unconscious processes** – e.g. unwitting power struggles, sabotage, games and/or collusion.

But what of the spirit in all of this? What is the primary informant to establishing 'win–win' contracts? In essence, the underlying purpose in contracting lies with our concern and care for the wellbeing of the client – his or her humanity, uniqueness, vulnerability and strengths. Our supervisees want their clients to succeed in whatever way they may choose and, as supervisors, we contribute to this process. For coaching to be effective, it is paramount that the relationship is underpinned by respect and trust – so the coach needs to be resourceful enough within him or herself to co-create this relationship.

## The contribution of the client organization

We also need to consider the role and contribution that the sponsoring organization makes and that may help or hinder our supervisees in co-creating ethical and professional working agreements with their client, in the best interests of the client, especially when we consider some of the ethical dilemmas we have discussed.

Huge sums of money are being invested in coaching by UK organizations. It is not unreasonable therefore that they seek a return on investment (ROI) and reassurance that the work that is being done is effective and justifiable, especially when, in some instances, the immediate results are not necessarily visible or evident.

With growing sophistication in terms of their understanding of coaching among the buyers, there is an emerging trend in the UK for organizations to insist on the coaches not only being qualified and/or accredited, but also that they can provide evidence of being 'in supervision'. And yet, those asking may not necessarily be entirely clear what they are asking for.

At a surface level, both quality control and reassurance play a part here for the organization as they seek coaches to meet this criterion, as it provides them with some assurance of the coach being both professionally and ethically effective.

However, what part could the organization play in creating the context for reducing the potential dilemmas that may emerge and that would support the coach to provide the best possible coaching?

▼ *"I don't know what's involved; nobody can explain clearly what it is, or that it's different from coaching the coach."*

▼ *"I'm afraid of being exposed (and shamed)."*

▼ *"I don't know how to find a supervisor."*

▼ *"I don't want to be seen to be less than expert, especially when I charge high fees."*

▼ *"I've spent a fortune on my training, so now that I know how to coach, I don't understand why I need supervision and I can't afford to pay for any additional or ongoing input."*

For many, it would appear that merely the term conjures up associations with 'parent–child', manager–employee and with it, the potential perhaps to tap into historic shame as learners, with a fear of exposure for 'not knowing'. At the same time, many coaches do use a range of means to support their wellbeing, such as participating in peer groups, co-coaching fora, workshops and Action Learning Sets.

## Our task as supervisors to support 'best practice'

As we know, the world of coaching and, indeed, any related practices that involve person-to-person engagement encompasses mental, psychological and emotional territory, so the safety and wellbeing of all participants, particularly the client, is paramount. At this point, with a good understanding of the contracting process, and familiarity with an ethical code, we can see that the coach is well placed to engage in generative, productive and effective coaching relationships that meet the description of 'best practice' and that enable their clients to address, if not completely achieve, all of their intended outcomes.

At the same time, it is almost inconceivable to me that each of us can be consistently 'perfect' as practitioners where human relationships are involved. No two relationships are the same, and the demands of the coaching process and relationship are high. As supervisors, we know that our supervisees can find themselves in unknown waters within a coaching session, so they need to have an ethical and professional underpinning to support their practice, and part of our purpose in supervision is to provide the safe forum where together we can explore the diverse dimensions of what may occur in any given assignment.

Equally, however skilful and experienced professional practitioners may be, we know that the impact of our own personal circumstances may unwittingly influence how we are able to show up at any given appointment. Thus, coaches cannot foresee the impact that they may have on their clients and how this may trigger significant psychological or emotional responses that may then show up not only in the coaching but also in our supervision sessions.

I now go on to examine our task as supervisors to support coaches' ethical practice and how we can insure that coaches are supported effectively.

Across the literature devoted to coaching supervision, three themes recur as the key functions of supervision:

▼ *formative, normative and restorative (Proctor, 1997)*

▼ *educational, supportive and managerial (Kadushin, 1976)*

▼ *developmental, resourcing and qualitative*
   *(Hawkins and Smith, 2006).*

From this we can see that supervision provides a forum for coaches to learn and develop through reflection on practice, to recharge their batteries through off-loading or sharing and resolving issues of concern, and to gain affirmation that they are practicing effectively, ethically and safely in the best interests of their clients and themselves. Within this, supervision allows the coach to explore, unravel and resolve many of the aforementioned ethical dilemmas that arise.

As a strong advocate of supervision myself, I am aware that I may be veering into sensitive territory when I suggest that supervision also holds a strong quality control element. At the risk of sounding like a 'critical parent' (Stewart and Joines, 1987), the key factor that informs my stance is the protection and wellbeing of the client, the client organization and the coach himself/herself.

## Creating the safe space in supervision

The question I find myself asking is how do we as supervisors create 'adult-adult' (Stewart and Joines, 1987) relationships in supervision that enable the coach to reflect, learn and recharge his or her batteries. When asked what they do when faced with some of the incidents we have discussed earlier, often coaches will say, "I take it to supervision" and do so with no sense of embarrassment or shame that they do not have all the answers. In the following examples below, we can see that the coach is willing to lay himself/herself bare, and our role as supervisor is to create that non-judgmental, unconditional positive regard for all parties. Together we can then explore and reflect together to understand, learn, grow and heal whatever it is that has emerged, be it through an ethical tension or, in some sense, an incomplete contract at the start.

At the same time, as a coaching supervisor, we have our own values and stance with some of the incidents that our coaches may bring to supervision. So, how do we help our coaches to develop their ethical awareness and fluency? We may invite the coach to be explicit about his or her values and how these may inform his or her responses with his or her clients 'in the moment' and we may share our own perspectives as the basis to expand the coach's choices and possible courses of action. One of our tasks in supervision is to support the coach to develop his or her own capability to make ethical decisions by increasing his or her ethical awareness, developing his or her capacity to determine a course of action and subsequently live with the ambiguities in whatever decisions he or she takes (Carroll and Gilbert, 2011).

*Examples of **"I take it to supervision"***

**COACH:** *"I take issues that I feel 'uncomfortable' about – where I'm not sure what is the best course of action to take or when I'm not sure how to respond – either because the incident is new to me, or I get a strong emotional or physical reaction when the issue arises, or when my own values are compromised and which may get in the way of the work or it's too complex to sort out in the moment i.e. there are too many perspectives or layers to consider all at once, I can't tease it out in the moment,"*

**FOR EXAMPLE:** A client admits that he is having an affair with a member of staff and he is thinking of leaving his wife and three children and this clashes with the coach's personal beliefs around marriage."

**COACH:** *"For me, supervision is a 'clean' space, totally separate from the different stakeholders (client, sponsor, line manager) where I can give further attention to the client – so, not just in the coaching session or when writing up notes – I feel a responsibility to that client to take him or her or the issue to supervision (even though the client may not see it as an issue)."*

**FOR EXAMPLE:** The client is being bullied or sexually harassed by his or her line manager and, unbeknownst to the client, is a colleague or sponsor of the coach.

**COACH:** *"Sometimes I'm not sure what is going on between me and the client – it just doesn't feel 'right' (e.g. unconscious processes at work – psychological games being played – old* *patterns being enacted) – so the ethical question for me is whether I'm doing the 'best job possible'. My supervisor helps me to explore whether there is an issue with my practice, my state, the client/state and/or the larger system – she does this with respect for me and the client, with curiosity, and with concern that we are both 'OK.'*

**AUTHOR:** *What makes it 'clean'?*

**COACH:** *'Not being judged. It's a space to be authentic, be who I really am, own up to my true thoughts and feelings, and then gain clarity about what belongs where, so then I can think more clearly about the issue and where it all belongs: with client, the sponsor, with me – I can sort out the ownership. I can then navigate a path through the different ingredients.'*

**FOR EXAMPLE:** considering the client who shares that he or she is being sexually harassed:

▼ *What is the corporate 'line' on harassment?*

▼ *What happens to whistleblowers in this organization?*

▼ *What 'level' of seriousness would mean that I would break confidentiality?*

▼ *What about my relationship with the perpetrator?*

▼ *What if the perpetrator found out that I was the one who went to HR?*

▼ *What is my opinion of that person now and how will I relate to him or her now I know what he or she has done?*

▼ *How do I deal with the fact that I too have been sexually harassed?*

**COACH:** *"When I have significant life events myself (e.g. personal relationship issues, major problems with my work or living space, other non-coaching experiences), I take these to supervision because I'm aware that these are affecting at some*

*level my capacity to be fully present with my client.*
*So, by sharing this with my supervisor, this gives me the head*
*and heart space to then engage with my client when I am with*
*him or her."*

## TOP TIP – deciding what to bring to supervision

From here we can establish that some of the reasons that determine
when and why a coach brings issues to supervision include:

▼ *the stage of development of the coach (Hawkins cited in*
*Passmore, 2011; Bachkirova, 2011)*

▼ *when the coach experiences discomfort either during or as a*
*result of a coaching session (e.g. a conflict of interest between*
*client and organization)*

▼ *when the coach experiences an emotional response*
*(transference or projection)*

▼ *where there is no definite 'right' or 'wrong' but a choice*
*needs to be made*

▼ *when there are choices to be made because several parties*
*are affected: the client, the sponsor, the line manager, the*
*organization and/or the coach*

▼ *when the coach needs a safe space where he or she can be truly*
*himself/herself, can explore these issues and he or she can gain*
*clarity in his or her thinking and feelings*

▼ *when life events may be getting in the way of the coach being*
*his or her very 'best'.*

## END NOTE – some questions still unanswered

There is one final area that we have not yet discussed and for which
I hold a number of questions if we are to become a fully fledged
profession. Again, at the risk of sounding like the 'critical parent',

at this stage in the development of our profession, while several of the coaching associations have published a complaints procedure (e.g. EMCC), there is no independent body where a client can take his or her concerns when he or she experiences what he or she believes to be 'unethical practice'. Equally, as supervisors, to whom do we refer or what do we do when we have serious concerns about a coach's capacity to practice ethically and professionally? And whose responsibility is it to call a practitioner to account?

**SUMMARY**

In this chapter we have identified and considered some of the ethical dilemmas that arise in the coaching relationship and the issues facing the coach when working in the complex domain of organizations. To this end, we have explored the importance of establishing robust coaching agreements that support all parties in the coaching assignment.

With the emergence of coaching as a profession we have discussed how the coaching associations support their members with ethical codes of practice and guidelines for supervision and how these are intended to protect and support the clients and the client organizations.

We have explored the role and purpose of supervision and how this practice supports the coach to provide a consistent and professional service in the best interests of his or her clients, while attending to his or her own wellbeing and development. I hope it is clear now how this dimension of ethical practice and contracting is closely aligned within the integral elements of the Full Spectrum Model.

## REFERENCES

**Allan, Julie (2011)** (Chapter 10) in Passmore, J (Ed) *Supervision in Coaching*, London, Kogan Page

**Bachkirova, T (2011)** *Developmental Coaching*, Berkshire, UK: McGraw Hill.

**Bennett, JL (2006)** "An agenda for coaching related research: a challenge for researchers", *Coaching Psychology Journal: Practice and research, 58(4)*: 240-249.

**Carroll, M (2009)** "Ethical maturity". Presentation to Centre for Supervision and Team Development (CSTD) and Bath Consultancy Group Graduate Groups, Bath, UK. (See www.bathconsultancygroup. com and www.cstd.co.uk)

**Carroll, M and Gilbert, M (2011)** *On Being a Supervisee: Creating Learning Partnerships*, London, Vukani Publishing 2005-2011.

**Coaching Supervision Academy (2013)** coachingsupervisionacademy.com/our-approach/full-spectrum-model (Last date of access 01 April 2013)

**European Mentoring and Coaching Council** (http://www.emccouncil.org.uk)

**(EMCC) UK Code of Ethics,(Updated 2008)** http://www.emccouncil.org./src/ultimo/models/Download/4. pdf_2012 (Last date of access 01 April 2013)

**Hawkins, P and Smith, N (2006)** *Coaching, Mentoring and Organizational Consultancy*, Berkshire, UK: McGraw Hill.

**Hawkins P, (2011)** (Chapter 10) in Passmore, J (Ed) *Supervision in Coaching*, London, Kogan Page

**Kadushin, A (1976)** *Supervision in Social Work*, New York, US: Columbia University Press.

**Lane, David, A, Stelter, Reinhard and Rostron, Sunny Stout** *The Future of Coaching as a Profession* (2010) in *The Complete Handbook of Coaching* (2010) Cox, Bachkirova and Clutterbuck (Eds), , London, UK: Sage (pp. 357-368).

**Lane, David,** A *Ethics and Professional Standards in Supervision* (2011) in *Coaching and Mentoring Supervision* (2011) Bachkirova, Jackson and Clutterbuck (Eds), Berkshire, UK: McGraw Hill (pp. 91-104).

**Proctor, B (1997)** *Contracting in Supervision,* (Chapter 12) in *Contracts in Counselling* (1997) Charlotte Sills (Ed), London, Sage Publications

**St John-Brooks, KD** What are the ethical challenges involved in being an internal coach?, International Journal of Mentoring and Coaching, Volume 5 Issue 1 June 2010

**Steare, Roger (2009)** *Ethicability*, UK: Roger Steare Publishing Ltd.

**Steiner, C (1974)** *Scripts People Live: Transactional analysis of life scripts*, New York, US: Grove Press.

**Stewart, I and Joines, V (1987)** *TA Today*, Nottingham, UK: LifeSpace Publishing.

**Townsend, C (2011)** (Chapter 9) in Passmore, J (Ed) *Supervision in Coaching*, London, Kogan Page

**Williams, P and Anderson, SK (2006)** *Law & Ethics in Coaching*, New Jersey, US: John Wiley & Sons.

# 2 | *Mind, body and metaphor*

- Jackie Arnold

## Abstract

THIS CHAPTER explores the way in which coach supervisors are able to create a safe space for supervision and nurture a genuine quality of present moment attention. This sits largely in the green part of the Full Spectrum Model where the focus is on energy management, presence and the internal supervisor. We attempt to show ways to be present in the here and now coming from a place of acceptance and non-judgment. By increasing our levels of attention it becomes possible to co-create a deep thinking space for the supervisee to reflect and grow. Research proves that mindfulness boosts happiness and wellbeing (Brown and Ryan, 2003).

It can also increase levels of attention and empathy for both supervisor and those seeking supervision.

This chapter will also cover the importance of our voice tone and pace in addition to the alignment of our body as coach supervisors. Case studies are provided to illustrate these key areas and to show the power of non-verbal language.

Finally we will introduce the clean language questions and the symbolic modeling work of psychotherapist David Grove, and of Penny Tompkins and James Lawley, who have been at the forefront of developing and promoting the application of Clean Language. A powerful intervention and a valuable skill for coach supervisors, it enables us to stand back from our work with as little interference as possible. It enables us to avoid making assumptions and allows the supervisee to explore his or her own unique worldview. In this way we can have the essential overview and contemplative approach needed when building strong relationships as coach supervisors. This forms part of the yellow spectrum of the FSM where we are focusing on building the supervision alliance. Together we will discover the power of exploring the metaphorical landscape that supports those we supervise. In this journey of discovery we have a unique glimpse into the world of our supervisee, creating a strong bond and a true supervision partnership.

**TIP**

When supervising at our best we need to create a connection with supervisees at a fundamentally deep level. This enables us to work on the true nature of the issues that arise and to achieve insights by means of safe exploration.

*"The inner self is revealed in the unconscious language and symbolic landscape of the supervisor and their supervisee."*

- Jackie Arnold, 2011

## What you will discover in this chapter:

▼ *how to create a safe space and mindful presence*
   *– for self and supervisee*

▼ *the power and importance of your voice*

▼ *the body and gestures in supervision*

▼ *clean language and symbolic modelling in coaching supervision.*

## A first discovery of true presence and stilling of the mind in action

I lived in Switzerland for fourteen years from 1972 to 1986. In Switzerland, high in the mountains, there are incredibly agile mountain goats. They climb in crevices and along ridges that would seem impossible to those gazing from below. In fact many people are unable to see them as they are so far away and so well camouflaged. In addition, there are tiny deer leaping from rock to rock and grazing on the rich grass far away from human habitation. Marmots are also hiding in the undergrowth, so shy that people often do not realize that they exist. There are, however, people who have no trouble hearing and seeing these creatures. The mountain people have trained themselves to practice a kind of mindful stillness. They are so aware of their own body, presence and surroundings that they are able to see and hear with a sharpness so elusive to others. It is this kind of stillness and acute connection with nature that creates this special bond. It is the energy of nature and all it offers us, if we just take the time to listen and observe. This is the kind of calm awareness that coach supervisors need when attending to the challenges and issues brought to our sessions. It is this kind of intense listening that is needed when practicing clean language as without it we may miss vital information and subtle nuances.

**CASE STUDY 1**

I was fortunate in that my father-in-law Toni had been a Swiss mountain guide from a very early age. From the first moment I met him I noticed how he observed and listened to anyone who spoke to him. He responded to the present moment with a profound sense of calm and deep awareness. He seemed to know instinctively what you needed without asking. If you were sad or happy, if you needed space or company, he would know, and with few words he was able to convey his love and quiet presence when needed.

He took us to the mountains on many occasions and his connectedness with nature was astounding. I remember feeling frustrated when I was unable to see and hear what he so easily saw and heard. Animals in the shady crevices, tiny mountain flowers, birds high in the sky, trickling water – he had no better hearing or sight, just mindful presence and oneness with all that surrounded him. Slowly I dropped my *wanting* to see and I saw a tiny movement. Quietly I observed emotions in my body and noticed my surroundings, just as they were and not as I had imagined. I became still and curious with *less expectation*. Images, sensations, feelings and sounds all began to have a clarity I had not known before.

**TIP**

In our work as coach supervisors being in this space of gentle curiosity, paying attention to what is present in that moment without internal 'chatter' is when the real shifts for the supervisee can occur.

It is in this space that we are able to develop our own intuition for good practice in supervision. We create the conditions to understand and learn what is effective and what may need our attention.

*"The success of an intervention depends on*
*the inner condition of the intervener."*

**- Senge et al., 2004**

In the Swiss mountains I began to discover a real moment-to-moment awareness of how everything was connected – a realization that all was as it needed to be, in that particular space and time. It was fascinating to realize that aspects of my own way of being had obscured what I felt, saw and heard. I wondered how many people walking through these mountains had missed seeing these delightful creatures in the wild or, if they had seen them, had taken the time to listen and observe.

Ideally as coach supervisors we are trained to sense and tap into another person's energy field. At the same time we need to be acutely aware of our own patterns of thought and energy flow. Only then are we able to put aside intrusions and focus entirely on the other person and their landscape, co-creating a particular transformative mindful space. We pay respectful attention to the body movements, the sighs, the breathing and the voice tone of the supervisee. This allows us to access our own intuition and to self-manage and trust that what arises in the session is there for a reason. Expectation and preconceived ideas about how the session should go are left at the door. We are patient and able to allow for the emergence of what comes. This can be challenging when the supervisee brings situations we can also identify with. It is useful to remember that no two people ever feel or experience similar issues in quite the same way. It is at these times that we need to refrain from entering into the content of the session and remain open to what unfolds. We also know that long after the sessions this transformative relationship is carried further. Supervisees are better able to reflect on their own learning and discoveries and take away new understanding to their own coaching practice. Only when nurturing this special connection, keeping out our own ego and intrusive thoughts, can our supervision be truly effective.

The practice of 'mindfulness' is one way that supervisors can increase awareness of what is present and be non-judgmental in sessions with supervisees. The Full Spectrum Model of supervision is aligned with the sentiment of 'mindfulness' in Theravada Buddhism, which is described as *Satipathana – Sati* being the element of awareness and Pathana being the element of keeping present.

So how do we as coaching supervisors access these elements, maintain their presence and rekindle the spirit of transformation? How do we manage to create safety for both coach and clients in the multiple relationships that often exist when supervising in large organizations?

When we tap into the silence that quietens us down, it enables us to go deeper into the soul of our sessions. It gives us the capability to 'hold' the different parts of the system and to be acutely aware of what is often *not* said. It insures that contractual boundaries are not crossed and that all stakeholders are respected.

How often do we feel the need to respond to the specific pain or challenge of our supervisees and in so doing do we intrude on *their* own way of being and coping? In this way we merely interrupt our supervision relationships, which form such a crucial part of the Full Spectrum Model. We can prevent this by increasing our awareness of how are we sitting with our clients – still, relaxed and open to whatever turns up, paying attention to our gestures and noticing how they fit with our words and emotions, noticing how our supervisees use words and noticing how their gestures and non-verbal language inform the emerging knowledge. It is this quality of attention that shows respect and that allows for an unconditional positive space for supervisees to explore and grow. It enables us to better notice and understand the intricacies and often multilayered relationships involved, to keep a broad overview of what goes on in organizations and how the different parts relate to one another and understand the different personality types and behaviors that affect standards, performance, wellbeing and core values. I liken this to the eye of a golden eagle hovering over the relationship, at a distance, acutely aware and holding the wider picture. Yet, being able to swoop down at a moment's notice to support when needed.

When we pay attention and are present in the 'now' of the session we can support supervisees to clarify their own understanding of those sometimes very complex contexts.

> *"The key to 'seeing from the whole' is developing the capacity not only to suspend our assumptions but to 'redirect' our awareness towards the generative process that lies behind what we see."*
>
> **- Senge et al., 2004: 42**

It is the quiet and respectful attention we show when listening to a wonderful musical performance. It is the kind of tingle that goes up the spine when the music fills our soul and the sound enables our mind to soar to unknown heights. When we consider all that supervisees bring to the sessions and how present with them we need to be, it is helpful to remember those times when we have also been moved and when we have been truly at one with our thoughts and emotions – to recall those moments that have touched our hearts and allowed us to go deeper to listen to the rhythm of the soul.

Is there a distinction between quietening our mind and presence? In the case study above my father-in-law was *mindful* of all that surrounded him. He was able to take in the sounds, sights, smells and touch and to be in tune with his feelings. He was *present* with his body and his breathing was totally grounded in the moment with no internal chatter or invasive thoughts.

## Try this relaxation exercise

Sit in a straight-backed chair and feel the chair against your back and legs. Keep your hands relaxed on your knees and do not cross your legs but keep them planted on the floor, knees slightly apart. Breathe a little more slowly and deeply using your 'out breath' to let chatter and intrusive thoughts float away. Use your 'in breath' to take in new calm energy. Do this slow breathing for a few minutes.

Now stiffen every muscle in your body. Start with the feet and work up the legs. Increase the tension in your arms and upper body. Feel the neck tighten and the muscles of the face contract. Realize that you are probably holding your breath. Also notice how much effort is going into keeping the muscles tight and the tension that is building. Now take a deep breath and relax your body, but only a little. Keep the tension in your face, neck and shoulders. Feel how uncomfortable this is. Be aware of the energy that you are using to keep these muscles tense.

Now breathing evenly, starting from your face muscles gradually relax your body. Take some deep breaths from the diaphragm (just under your rib cage). Relax your shoulders and arms as you breathe and feel the tension draining out of you as you slowly move downwards through the legs and feet. Feel the clothes on your body. Be aware of the material as it moves against your skin. Feel the hard back and seat of the chair. Are you sure that your shoulders have remained relaxed? Are your neck and throat soft and free of tension?

If you find it hard to relax, try visualizing yourself in a calm place that you know well. 'Take' yourself there in your mind and feel the atmosphere, smell the air, see the surroundings. Allow yourself to just 'be' there in this familiar place for a while. Close your eyes or look out of the window. If any intrusive thoughts enter your mind let them float into the rubbish bin, or out of the window. Feel and notice how it is to be in this calm and easy state. Enjoy the freedom of your own 'present' minutes. This exercise will help you to manage your own energy (FSM) before meeting with your supervisees.

**CASE STUDY 2**

### Supervision session three – the place of 'not knowing'

In this case study we will look at one of a series of three coaching supervision sessions (session three of six) that will illustrate the importance of bodily presence and 'staying with' the supervisee.

This coach was a highly experienced business executive wishing to develop her own coaching practice. She was also managing the transition to coach from a successful career as a lawyer. She was motivated and wanted to use supervision to enhance her coaching style and build her practice. After the first two sessions where clear contracting had been agreed and the sessions planned with a suitable venue identified, a pattern began to emerge.

## Supervision session 3

*Full Spectrum Model in practice*

We had built a trusting relationship over the first two sessions and this was demonstrated by the coach being able to use the space for reflection and thinking time. At the beginning of the third session it was apparent, however, that the coach had not been able to align her previous role with that of her new role as a coach. She was fearful (her words) of stepping out of her 'safe' environment into one that appeared totally new and unknown. It is often challenging to 'stay with' a supervisee in the space of not knowing. However, in my experience it is at these crucial junctions that mindfulness and presence are at their most powerful. Exploring the fear and staying out of the supervisee's way using clean language during this exploration proved to be a real turning point. As I listened I allowed my thoughts and feelings to float around and above the supervisee and just noticed what was occurring. (The eye of the eagle hovering above.)

Using a basic clean language question (see below for clean questions) I asked if there was *anything else* about this fear she had identified and if it had a size or shape (prompting her to move to a symbolic perception). There was a long silence and then she told me that the fear was a pink blob at the front of her forehead.

(I remember noticing a fleeting thought that (for me) pink was a strange color for a fear and later reflected on how wonderful it is to be constantly surprised by others' views of the world, so different to our own – perhaps I came out of presence for a moment …)

I breathed deeply, re-centered myself and asked her what kind of blob this was when it was 'pink and at the front of her forehead'. She replied that it was like a piece of 'rubber' that could be different shapes. As I listened I had no idea where she was in her thoughts or feelings, all I did was stay with her in her metaphorical landscape, both with my energy and the slow pace of my voice. She explored her fear and noticed more about it in response to my questions. With some reflecting back of her own words she began to realize that she had control of the 'pink rubber'. She could take it and put it where she chose. She moved her hands as if she was taking the pink blob and placing it in front of her. As I directed her attention to her gestures she said it felt as if this had given her back the power that she had lost. The fear was no longer 'looking over her shoulder' as before but out there in front where she could see it. To explore this metaphor further I asked her when the pink blob was where she could see it, and it was no longer looking over her shoulder, and she had the power back … what happened then? After a longish pause and a few further questions she said that her fear was no longer in control of her. She realized the only person who was able to hold her back was herself. She then spoke about her coaching practice with renewed enthusiasm and identified specific ways forward for the coming weeks.

In this session the space of 'not knowing' created a catalyst for a real shift of energy for the supervisee. This was unfamiliar territory in that she was encouraged to visualize her fear as something tangible/visual and to explore it in a totally new way. She had no notion of where the pink rubbery fear had come from. She had merely discovered that she had a choice: to allow it to stop her from moving forward or to put it where she could see and control it.

At the end of the session I asked myself, "Was I at ease during this supervision session in my place of not knowing?" and "Was there a time when I wanted to know what was going on for my supervisee?" as well as "How did I manage to 'just be' during this session?"

I recall a quote from Eckhart Tolle in *The Power of Now* where he says that if we "remove time from the mind – it stops", in essence saying that being present in the now is all we need in order to still our thoughts. We experience the kind of stillness in unknown territory that captures the brief moments so vital in our work with others.

In this case study the power of investigating the metaphorical landscape of the supervisee allowed essential new knowledge to emerge.

> **TIP** In our work as coach supervisors being in this space of gentle curiosity, paying attention to what is present in that moment without internal 'chatter', is when the real shifts for the supervisee can occur.

## The use of voice and body

Being present also means paying calm attention to your voice and gestures. Voice plays a key role both in our coaching and our supervision sessions. The stress we put on words and the specific intonation can reveal so much about the intention of the facilitator. If we use a neutral tone of voice and sensitive inquiry, it enables the supervisee to decide for himself/herself where to put the emphasis or intonation. It keeps us from making assumptions. There are a variety of ways to say, for example, "What exactly do you value most about this situation?" or "What kind of intervention was helpful to you?"

Our voice can be gentle and curious or it can have specific emphasis on 'what' or on 'you' in either question. Sometimes the stress or intonation is unconscious and our feelings or opinion show through even though we may not realize it. The neutral tone and calm inquiry enables the supervisee to decide for himself/herself where to put the emphasis or intonation.

When supervising as natural *listeners, we open our inquiry from the inside out, from a genuine place of* curiosity. We show through our voice and gestures a non-judgmental tone that encourages easy thoughts that flow unhindered.

Try this the next time you supervise (with the permission of your supervisee):

The best way to hear how we sound is to record our voice during a session. This has astonishing results and can really reveal hidden nuances. It shows clearly where we put our emphasis and can transform our way of connecting in sessions. Next time you supervise let your supervisee know you are recording the session and emphasize that this is for your own learning and growth.

We often hear in supervision that coaches can be fearful of asking the 'right' questions or using the 'correct' models. This fear can seriously damage the relaxed relationship between coach and client and the voice and body language will also suffer. When we are fearful our vocal cords tighten and our body stiffens. Often we are not aware of these small changes. Taking a breath and getting used to the silence, staying with the unknown and stilling the mind can go a long way to staying relaxed and calm. (See the previous exercise on relaxation.)

**Try this now:**

These breathing exercises will enhance breathing capacity and create a relaxed and easy body flow. We can do these alone or ideally with a colleague:

1. To help abdominal awareness, person *A* lies on his or her back on the floor. (Some people may need a small book under the head.) The other person, person *B*, places a book on *A*'s diaphragm. *A* relaxes his or her whole body and concentrates on the book as it rises and falls with each breath. *A* flattens the abdomen as much as possible on the 'out' breath. *B* watches to make sure that the whole body is relaxed and the only movement is the book on the abdomen. Change places and repeat.

2. Stand next to your partner and check that your shoulders are relaxed. Inhale only, with five short gasps (HA HA HA HA HA) with your mouth open. Notice the movement in your diaphragm. Then exhale with five quick puffs (HU HU HU HU HU). Next try the same exercise with your mouth closed and taking the inhale gasps and exhale puffs through your nose.
   *Note: It may be easier to place your hands on your diaphragm – also watch that the shoulders stay soft and relaxed.*

3. Now, facing your partner, exhale all your breath until you feel completely empty and then inhale taking a full deep abdominal breath. (Try to stay relaxed.) Repeat three times each. (Partners should watch for moving or stiffened shoulders.)

4. Inhale to half your capacity and hold your breath for 20 seconds – and then exhale gently. Repeat this over several days increasing the time until it reaches a full minute. This will strengthen your breathing and the related muscles.

5. Exhale with a laugh. HA HA HA HA. Feel this in your abdominal muscles, then gently inhale and repeat. (Keep a watch on your partner for any stiffness or raised shoulders. Test this by placing your hands on his or her shoulders as he or she laughs.)

6. Stand with your hands on your hips. Lean slightly back and look up towards the ceiling. Let yourself yawn and feel your waist expand and your diaphragm flatten. As you exhale say, "AH" for as long as you can remain relaxed and at ease.

Done regularly we can enhance our vocal tone and be more relaxed before and after sessions.

**TIP**

Professional singers do these exercises as a matter of course. As coaches and supervisors we use our voice as a vital part of our job and thus for us they are also essential.

**CASE STUDY 3**

I recently had the privilege of attending a demonstration by Monty Roberts, the famous 'horse whisperer'. Monty has spread his unique, non-violent method of breaking in horses throughout the world and his voice is a vital part of the process. He is truly in the moment as soon as he approaches the horses and his voice takes on a calmness and a gentle persuasive edge at different moments during the process. He uses his voice and his gestures in such a way as to keep control, while at the same time allowing the horses their own time to 'join up' with him.

In this demonstration the first horse he works with is a big, seventeen hands, truly wild stallion. He needs to remain totally in the moment as one false move could be dangerous. Every movement and gesture he makes is deliberate and he mirrors the horse so that the connection between them develops and grows before your eyes. Monty calls it understanding their language and their world. He is mindful of the horse's eye and ear movements and the angle at which he holds his body so the horse feels safe. He creates a place of strong presence and calm. As you watch you can see the relationship growing and the horse beginning to trust.

As the horse becomes aware that Monty poses no threat and is behaving in a way he understands he starts to connect. He slows his pace and allows Monty to approach, and before your eyes you witness a large stallion taking the bridle for the first time. This is a truly magical experience and one I will never forget.

Gestures and non-verbal clues mirror our innermost thoughts. Our gestures give away what we really feel and so paying attention to them in the here and now can help us to relax and become centered. Often supervisees are not aware of the gestures they make and our gently bringing their attention to them can have dramatic results. One supervisee kept looking and unconsciously nodding at a corner of the room while he was speaking. When I mirrored his movement and asked him what he was nodding to in the corner, he was surprised and realized that it was his partner who he wanted to involve in his coaching business going forward. When we delved further and I slowly asked *what kind of involvement* this would be, he became animated as he revealed several clear ideas for collaborative discussion.

It has long been accepted in the coaching and supervision world that voice and gestures play a vital part in sessions. Vocal tone and stress can be used consciously both to calm and to motivate coaching clients and supervisees. In NLP we are aware of how revealing eye movements and body language can be, but how do we express awareness and presence through voice and gestures?

Being aware of how our voice sounds in different situations, recording and listening to our own voice during sessions can be really revealing. When we are breathing and in the moment, our voice will attain a rich quality unlike the tones we use in everyday speech. We will naturally match those of the supervisee and blend in so that our voice becomes unobtrusive and yet supportive in tone and rhythm. We will unconsciously use the curious tone of voice that aids gentle inquiry, reflecting and staying with the language of the supervisee. In this way we need to do very little, merely listen and create that flowing energy that allows our supervisee to choose his or her own path forward.

*The human voice is the primary medium of communication in human beings. It is an expression of who we are and how we feel. In the timbre of a person's voice you can hear the subtle music of feeling and thought – the ever-shifting collage of emotions to which we are all prey.*

**- Developer of voice movement therapy Paul Newham**

## Clean language

Clean language was devised by psychotherapist David Grove, as a way to keep his assumptions out of his interactions with his clients, as far as possible, so he could work directly with their perceptions. It consists of 30 or so questions, asked in a curious way and with a particular tone of voice. The pace and timbre of the voice is a key element in the effectiveness of clean language questions. When faced with strong feelings or emotions our physiology changes. Our breathing is shallow and our thoughts can become muddled. The slow pace and brevity of clean questions enables supervisees to delve safely into the situations they bring to sessions. It frees the chatter and allows for mindfulness to occur. This slowing down and coming into the present moment is enhanced by the pauses between our questions and the reflecting back of the supervisee's exact words. It is as if the supervisor and supervisee are floating on the same wave, matching the other as the session flows back and forth. It is also very challenging for the supervisee as he or she is required to take ownership of his or her thought patterns and own metaphorical landscape.

We deliver clean language questions slower than at our normal pace and use a slightly deeper tonality. If when recording our sessions we feel that the tone of our voice could be deeper the vocal exercises above will help.

When I worked for BBC radio I needed to lower the tone of my voice for broadcasting and I managed to do this quite easily, which I found surprising. When we use clean language there is an implied sense of curiosity and we match the supervisee's *idiosyncratic* pronunciation and emphasis without seeming forced or intrusive. We can also use the NLP practices of pacing (matching the vocal pace of the supervisee) and leading (sometimes using voice and tone to bring a supervisee to a more productive/creative/quiet or reflective space) in a very sensitive and intuitive way.

It is worth noting that all the clean language questions begin with 'and' and they focus on the supervisee's 'perceptual present'. This allows the supervisee to continue the train of thought without interruption. (See the case study and diagram below.)

The 'nine-question compass' model (see Figure 2.1) was first published in the spring 1997 issue of *Rapport*: It is now published in *Metaphors in Mind* by Penny Tompkins and James Lawley (2005).

**LOCATING IN SPACE**

Where/whereabouts?
Does ... have size or shape?

**EVOLVING TIME**

What happens next?
Then what happens?

**DEFINING ATTRIBUTES**
What kind of ... ?
Anything else?

What happened just before?
Where did ... come from?

That's a ... like what?

**PULLING BACK TIME**

**SHIFTING SYMBOL**

**Figure 2.1** - *The original nine-questions compass (Note: "..." are the client's exact words.)*

As clean language is very flexible, what started out as a therapeutic process is now used in many contexts including coaching supervision. If you have heard of clean language before then it's likely that you'll also have heard of symbolic modeling. This is the name given by Penny Tompkins and James Lawley in their book *Metaphors in Mind* to the model they devised after working with and observing David Grove over several years. They wanted to discover what he was doing to achieve such good results. They combined David's ideas with ideas from the fields of cognitive linguistics, systems thinking and NLP to produce a model that could be taught to others to enable them to achieve the same kinds of results as David.

When using clean language in coaching supervision it is particularly useful to develop the metaphors that supervisees use naturally as they speak. By asking coaching questions it helps to slow the supervisee down and enables them to think about the meaning and words they have used. When the supervisor reflects the words of the supervisee it subtly builds the special relationship that underpins the Full Spectrum Model as the supervisee feels supported in his or her own space. Their metaphors are unique and as they are developed the supervisee unconsciously feels understood. He or she feels that his or her own view of the situation has been acknowledged.

Linguist George Lakoff and philosopher Mark Johnson wrote in *Metaphors We Live By*: "The essence of metaphor is understanding and experiencing one kind of thing in terms of another."

We all use metaphors as part of our daily lives. They are very familiar to us and form part of who we are. It is very revealing to notice the metaphorical world you inhabit and how that differs from those around you. You may be unaware of how frequently you use metaphors on a daily basis.

Here are some metaphors that you may be familiar with:

▼ *I'm banging my head against a brick wall.*

▼ *We're up against it this month.*

▼ *Take your time over that.*

▼ *He got a glowing report.*

▼ *She's full of confidence.*

▼ *I need to build my skills.*

▼ *Coaching supervision is growing.*

▼ *Which branch of the business do you work in?*

It is when you develop these metaphors that supervisees really delve deep into their visual landscape. Often their perception of the problem or situation begins to change. They come up with ideas and solutions that have previously *lain* hidden and are suddenly *in the spotlight*. Sometimes supervisees use their metaphors to notice how they deal with others or use specific language. It can be most illuminating. One supervisee described his situation in a company as that of "a lion trainer trying to tame the lions". When he noticed and investigated this further, he realized that his vision of his clients may not have been helpful or appropriate.

**Try this now:**

If you have a recording of a one-to-one meeting or supervision or coaching session listen to it, paying specific attention to your metaphors. Then ask yourself the clean questions in the diagram above to see what new knowledge emerges. Then repeat the process listening to the metaphors of your supervisee and see what clean questions you may have asked of their metaphors.

Sarah Green is the managing director of a local web design and marketing company. Sarah has built this business over the past 10 years and has had to face considerable challenges along the way. She trained as a coach to enhance her leadership skills and to enable her to coach her direct reports.

I first supervised Sarah (using some clean language) two years ago. During one session, she spoke about one of her staff as "buzzing all over the place". I decided to ask a few questions to develop this metaphor.

**QUESTION:** *"And when buzzing ... what kind of buzzing is that when it's all over the place?"*

**RESPONSE:** *"It's like there are ideas like bees flying round his head and they're out of control. I like the ideas he brings but feel he needs to be more in control, focus on one at a time before we all get stung."*

**QUESTION:** *"And you like the ideas he brings and feel he needs to be more in control ... and is there anything else about that control?"*

**RESPONSE:** *"Yes, I'd like to feel more in control when he comes with so many bees but it's also supporting him to stay focused."*

I then asked clean language questions of each subsequent response and each symbolic representation was explored. This helped Sarah to continually expand her awareness of her metaphoric landscape.

Developing this metaphor further led Sarah to take more time with her direct report in his next coaching session.

She realized that she had been rushing the sessions at the end of the day and in a subsequent supervision session she told me: "I like getting his ideas now. While some bees are still flying about, they are fewer and he can catch them. He also came up with the idea of sending me bullet points and now I am nowhere near as worried about coping with his ideas as I was."

And in the next session: "I am eager to find out how I can support him further. The bees are still a little bit elusive. I need a hive to contain them, more structure. He is such a rich source of inspiration and I do not want to dampen his enthusiasm; however, we could all get stung if the bees aren't contained."

I asked Sarah what needed to happen for "the hive to contain them and have more structure so she could support him further without getting stung" (taking care to use her own words and to match her voice tone).

She sat for a few minutes thinking and it was obvious that she needed time and space. During this time I was hovering above (using my eagle metaphor) and mindful of my breathing, keeping still yet attentive. She finally responded: "I need to get more organized in the office and to put a structure around the way we handle meetings. I need to delegate some of the work so that I can devote more time to the one-to-one coaching sessions and to team meetings. They need to feel I am taking time to listen to them. Then I can motivate them to take on more responsibility. Yes that feels right and that way we will definitely avoid getting stung."

I encouraged her to speak about the above plans in more detail – and with these in place Sarah felt more in control of what was happening while giving her direct reports the coaching support they needed.

In this next example of clean language the focus is on the body language of the supervisee and how often small gestures or facial expressions can be explored.

In a subsequent supervision session with Sarah she was describing a period where she had been team coaching. She spoke about how the team was beginning to communicate more effectively, yet progress had been slow. During her explanation Sarah was unconsciously tapping her fingers on the table to her left, and as it was quite frequent and noticeable I asked her a clean language question about her hand movement, so I asked... And when (and I tapped on the table as she was) is there anything else about (and I tapped again) Sarah looked down at her hands and there was quite a long period of silence. "Oh was I tapping my fingers? Yes … I suppose that shows how frustrated I am that they are not putting these strategies into practice as fast as I had hoped. Umm …perhaps I have been unconsciously demonstrating my impatience! However, I know that people need time to embed new ways of working so I need to allow them time, yes that's been useful bringing that to conscious awareness."

I asked Sarah if there was anything else about 'being patient'. She explained that she is someone who is an activist and realizes that others need time to think things through. She said that actually seeing herself tapping on the table had made her aware of her feelings of frustration and that she needed to grant her team a little slack.

We then explored what kind of 'patient' that was when it gave her team 'a little slack'. Sarah identified how she may encourage the members of her team without the pressure she had previously been putting on them. As I had noticed how she changed her facial expression from a frown to a smile when she used the word 'encouraging' I shared this with her by asking: "And when you (I frowned) and then you (I smiled) is there anything else about that smile when you are encouraging and giving them slack?" Sarah responded: "Oh – did I do that. Umm … actually I am probably not encouraging enough generally. This has really made me think about my own communication. I know I show on my face what I am feeling – I'll have to watch that from now on."

I then asked Sarah what it was that she felt she was like when she was working at her best with her team (encouraging her to think about a possible metaphor for her working at her best). She surprised herself by saying: "I really think that I am like my dog. He is very patient but is no walkover and he enjoys company and having people around him. He can motivate people by gently nudging them if he needs something without being aggressive. Oh and he is a very good listener."

The session ended with a lighthearted exploration into this metaphor to really embed the feeling of what 'working at your best' really meant for Sarah.

**TIP**

Getting fluent in clean language and symbolic modeling takes time and patience. Just use what you feel comfortable with and keep it simple.

The benefits of using clean language in coaching supervision are that we enable supervisees to think and reflect on their behavior and actions without language interference. We help them to own the metaphors they come up with and take them away for further reflection. The ideas that supervisees generate through the use of metaphor are generally quite inventive and idiosyncratic. They stay with the supervisee who generates them and provide an anchor a long time after the sessions. Supervisees get to understand the structure of their own thinking and behavior patterns and how this impacts on their clients. After a while, they learn how to pay attention to their own patterns and behavior as they occur, and they can work out ways to change those particular patterns that are not serving them. They glean knowledge about their own subjective experience and ways of being. In addition, since as a supervisor you are only using their words combined with the clean language questions, there is nothing for them to resist. You are just co-creating an energy and exploration that feels right for them. It increases their self-awareness and provides the support for exploration into the complex areas of their work covered by the Full Spectrum Model of supervision.

**TIP**

Try asking your supervisees this question slowly:

*"When you are coaching/working at your best, you're like ... what?"*

- *Working at Your Best,* Caitlin Walker Training Attention Ltd

## My own experience

When I had my own metaphors explored by my clean supervisor Marian Way of Clean Learning, I often came up with circles. Quite often the sun was part of the picture and I frequently mentioned yellow and gold. Nature played a part in my symbolic landscape, for example, the sea, its tides and its variety of moods. On one occasion I used a tree as the basis for building my new website. The tree had extended branches and I cut them down from six to three. These images have stayed with me and enabled me to relate to my experiences on a much deeper level.

As a coach supervisor I keep my image of a golden eagle. I visualize myself hovering above, keeping the bigger picture and yet being able to swoop down to support and challenge when needed. This helps me to keep my distance and reminds me to stay calm and focused. It also allows me to focus on all that surrounds my supervisee so that I am operating above the issues, not directly involved in them.

As a supervisor, try asking yourself this question: "When I am supervising at my best, what is it that I feel I am like?" See if you can create a powerful image for yourself as a supervisor.

When we ask Clean Language questions it encourages a heightened state of self-awareness, a sense of connecting with uncovered aspects of ourselves. If we can show others how to tap into the richness of their unconscious in a balanced mindful state, this is where real transformation happens. Supporting others to find their own metaphors is infinitely fascinating and revealing. It takes them to previously unexplored places, as in the case study above. It enables them to take away a powerful image that is a part of their own identity.

My supervisee is the owner of a coaching and training business. He employs several coaches/trainers and has developed a very close relationship with one of his staff. They have been close friends for more than 10 years. Now that my supervisee is downsizing he needs to let his close friend and employee go. He wants to be supportive but he feels that it will be difficult for his friend to find other employment as he is in his mid-50s. As his supervisor I work mainly with the challenges and client situations he brings but also with the management of his business and staff.

I asked my supervisee (Alan) if he would like to try a different approach using image and metaphor. I explained that this way of working could throw a different light on the relationship and may assist him in his exploration. He was very willing to do this and I then explained a little about how clean language worked by asking questions in a specific way to encourage the use of metaphor.

I asked him several clean questions about the relationship between himself and his employee (Tom). We continued the session for about half an hour and then, using his words, I asked, "As the relationship is close and you need to let Tom go, that's a relationship like … what?" (encouraging an image to emerge).

Alan looked off into the distance and slowly replied that the relationship was like two bikes riding side by side but that he felt that they were about to go down different paths. He could see that one path (his own) was fairly smooth and easy to ride down while the other (Tom's) was full of stones, was overgrown and was generally difficult.

I noticed how he had really frowned when describing the difficult path and how this had made him tense. He also used gestures to show the stony path. After reflecting back his words and gestures, yet wanting to encourage a desired outcome, I asked Alan what he wanted to have happen in this situation. His answer surprised him. He said that he wanted to clear the path for his friend so that he could ride on easily. He began to explain various ideas he had that he felt he could put in place so Tom would feel supported. His face lit up and he said he could also ask a member of his team to give him some exit coaching. He realized he had been focused on his idea of a tough ride in the future for Tom and had not seen what was possible for him right now.

During the session we developed more specifically how he may clear the path as well as how he would involve Tom in the clearing process. Alan said that this image of how they would clear the path would help him to let Tom go. He realized that instead of focusing on the redundancy he would listen to Tom's concerns and find out what ideas Tom had going forward. We developed his metaphor further to discover what kind of path he would provide for Tom. The path then became smoother and longer as he saw them co-creating an exit plan. Alan decided that he would be encouraging while ensuring that he did not take on all of the responsibility. This redundancy no longer felt as if he was pushing his friend along a rough path. Instead Alan recognized it as an unavoidable decision that had arisen due to the economic climate and felt that together they would see it through.

This more meditative approach to supervision allows images and reflections to come into play that may otherwise remain hidden. It offers another dimension to our work by encouraging the supervisee to enter a more contemplative state. In this state the unconscious mind can reveal images, allowing transformation to occur. By inviting the supervisee to enter into this mindful state and by explaining the process we will both enjoy a rich, rewarding experience.

It is worth mentioning here that one of the joys of this approach is the deep learning experienced by the supervisor. As professionals we learn and grow from our supervisees as we observe their challenges and discoveries. We will never know for sure how the minds of our supervisees are working. They inhabit different realities and they are influenced by different beliefs and cultures. The way we deal with an issue may not be the right method for those we supervise. It would be intrusive to impose our own ways of working and being mindful and present allows us to take a more objective stance. Just to notice their inner experience, withholding judgment and our own ideas allows us to develop our own skills further. It broadens our horizons and shows us ways of being we have never before encountered. It is indeed a privileged position and we can always be surprised by the paths we are led to discover.

## A coaching supervision tool

One NLP technique is useful for allowing supervisees to see things from different perspectives. In this way we can allow the supervisee to view the situations, relationships, challenges, and so forth from a variety of positions. This enables the supervisee to 'place himself/herself' in the positions described below. It allows him or her to get an objective view and to reflect and inhabit the different perspectives.

The first position is the perceptual position of ourselves: what we see, hear, feel, taste and smell, plus what we believe, our capabilities, our behaviors, and so forth.

Here we ask the supervisee to place himself/herself where he or she feels comfortable and to describe the situation from the coach's viewpoint.

The second perceptual position is that of another. The 'another' can be a person, an animal, a vegetable or a mineral and it can be real, imagined or remembered. It could be a character from a novel or a movie, a supportive mentor or a coach, or any number of archetypal roles.

Here we ask the supervisee to position himself/herself as if he or she was the 'another' – usually the client – in relation to where he or she has placed himself/herself. Then we ask him or her to reflect on and describe the situation from this viewpoint. It is important that he or she *becomes the 'another'* and speaks as if he or she were the 'another' – not as an observer.

The third perceptual position is of an observer. An observer can be a fair witness, real or imagined, with the ability to perceive in a non-judgmental and well-intentioned way.

Here we again ask the supervisee to take on the persona of the observer and to reflect and describe what he or she sees, feels, hears and knows about the situation/issue/challenge from this position.

The forth perceptual position is of the larger system or systems. The system (that can also be the organization) can see all of the other positions at once, as in the bigger picture, and they can perceive such things as relationships between other positions, effects on the system itself and systems within systems to any level of magnitude, large or small.

Once the supervisee has taken the first three positions we encourage him or her to take a helicopter view and to notice and reflect on what he or she can now see, hear, feel and know about this situation (that could be from the organizational perspective or whatever he or she feels is appropriate).

The final step is to take the supervisee back to his or her first position as coach and to ask him or her what he or she now sees, hears, feels and knows from here.

This is a very effective tool for coaching supervision as it allows the supervisee to experience and embody the client situation. It gives him or her an insight into the world of the client and the organization and often throws light on otherwise hidden corners of the issues/situation/relationships/ethics/contract.

Finally letting go of our own fear of making the right intervention or asking the right question will greatly enhance the process. When we are mindful of our own chatter and when we are able to relax and let go to let come, we become physically still and more attuned to the present moment. Our confidence returns and we produce the quiet energy highlighted by the FSM that is so vital to the coaching supervision process. Using clean language is masterful in allowing us to stand back, observe and respectfully challenge when appropriate.

> If we focus on our own anxieties and constantly
> wonder if we are 'good enough' as supervisors we
> will stifle our growth. Instead we should focus on the
> incredible learning journey that supervision provides.

The questions and interventions all arise from the supervisee and his or her words. When this is done with courage and moment-to-moment awareness, there is a fluidity and simplicity in the way that images occur. We journey together, co-creating this safe, reflective space while discovering other landscapes and while adding new learning and perspectives.

## REFERENCES

**Brown, Kirk Warren and Ryan, Richard M (2003)** The benefits of being present: 1/mindfulness and its role in psychological wellbeing, *Journal of Personality and Social Psychology by the American Psychological Association, Inc. 84(4)*: 822-884.

**Lawley, James and Tompkins, Penny (2005)** *Metaphors in Mind*, The Developing Company Press, Anglo-American Book Company Ltd, Carmarthenshire UK.

**Senge, Peter, Scharmer, C Otto, Jaworski, Joseph and Flowers, Betty Sue (2004)** *Presence*, Random House, New York.

## FURTHER READING

**Allan, Julie, Hawkins, Peter and Passmore, Johnathon (2011)** *Supervision in Coaching*, Kogan Page, London.

**Arnold, Jackie (2008)** *Coaching for Leaders in the Workplace*, How to Books, Oxford.

**Bachkirova, Tatiana, Jackson, Peter and Clutterbuck, David (2011)** *Coaching and Mentoring Supervision*, McGraw Hill, Berkshire and New York.

**Carroll, Michael and Gilbert, Maria C (2005)** *On Being a Supervisee*, Vukani Publishing, London.

**Glickstein, Lee (1998)** *Be Heard Now*, New York, US: Broadway Books.

**Sullivan, Wendy and Rees, Judy (2008)** *Clean Language*, Crown House Pub Ltd, Wales and CT USA.

# 3 | *Heart to heart*
*- a meeting place for*
*transformational learning*

- Samuel P. Magill Sr.

## Introduction

THE PURPOSE of this chapter is to explore and equip supervisors with a basic understanding of the benefit and approaches for working from their hearts. Although there are many references to "working from the heart", there is less information available on exactly what that means and how a supervisor may do it. Far more than a poetic metaphor, working from the heart can be a discipline requiring preparation and specific practices during supervision.

A parallel purpose will be to help supervisees and other parties to the supervision contract prepare and allow themselves to work from their hearts as well. This work is first and foremost a partnership. It applies to supervision of external coaches and perhaps even more so to supervision of internal coaches who are constantly immersed in the tensions of their organizations.

We will first examine the phenomena of being open hearted so that transformational learning can occur. Then we will explore how we may prepare to work in this way, questions that arise and the risks and benefits to the supervisor and the supervisee.

Throughout the chapter we will identify parts of the Full Spectrum Model that relate to the unfolding of the case study. The Full Spectrum Model includes both the more technical work of supervision such as multiparty contracting and the personal work of self-awareness and relationship building.

## Why is this chapter important?

The suggestion that there is benefit to both supervisor and supervisee is central to the propositions here. While these two people have their respective roles and responsibilities during supervision, there comes a point when there is no longer leader and follower, guide and student, more experienced and less experienced, higher and lower. At the moment when hearts really open, there is an astounding equality of personhood, a welcoming of one into the other, a merging of experiences. Both are students and both are teachers: two people combined as explorers.

Otto Scharmer suggests that intelligence of the heart is available "to us when we cultivate our capacity to appreciate and love". In the words of Humberto Maturana, "Love is the only emotion that enhances our intelligence." An open heart allows us to see and understand in ways that our cognition just doesn't get.

An even more subtle aspect of supervision heart to heart is healing. If we think of health as wholeness, and supervision aims to recreate wholeness of the coach with him or herself, then supervision has much to do with health and one of the most important benefits of coaching supervision for both internal and external coaches is the resourcing of the coach.

The kind of supervision being presented in this book has strong currents of healing in it: healing for the coach receiving supervision, healing for the client because of being heard more clearly and healing as a by-product for the supervisor who is constantly, always, just another human being working on his or her work.

**TIP**

If you are an internal coach, establish regular supervision, preferably with an external supervisor.

Why? At the beginning of my coaching practice I was in a very large aerospace company. An early mentor, Bob Duggan, suggested that I open my door, wait and see who walked in. Repeatedly, internal coaches, consultants and managers walked in to talk. They walked out resourced and more able to robustly carry on their work. That is a kind of soulful healing.

Our emphasis on the heart is more than a romantic notion. Current research on neuroanatomy, as reported in *Mindsight*, by Daniel Seigel, MD suggests that we are "hard wired to connect with one another". Research demonstrates, "how crucial it is to our development to have at least some relationships that are attuned, in which we feel we are held within another person's internal world, in their head and in their heart – relationships that help us thrive and give us resilience".

In its entirety, the Full Spectrum Model offers the possibility of healthy coaches who are worthy of their clients and able to hold their supervisees in exactly this fashion.

## What does it feel like to work from the heart?

As illustrated in the case study below, moments of heart connectedness have a very special quality. The experience is of an effortless timelessness with an unusually keen yet soft awareness. It is not as if we have escaped to a magical heart world; the very world we live in becomes more vibrant and very still. It seems that very few words need to be spoken to create understanding. Strangely, these moments can be welcomed, they can be anticipated and prepared for, but not exactly planned. It is not as if we say to one another, "Now, let's work from our hearts. Ready, Set, Open." It is much more like the experience of the children in CS Lewis's *Lion, the Witch and the Wardrobe* (1950), when the children are simply exploring a wardrobe, slowly going into its depths, and then suddenly find themselves in another world. In that place, for however long we are there, we are able to attend to our work in very special ways.

As French mathematician Blaise Pascal famously said: The heart has reasons that reason will never understand. Far from a poetic statement, we now know the heart does indeed do its own reasoning. Daniel Siegel, M.D. works with current research in neurobiology and in his recent book, Mindsight, writes "It is important to remember that the activity of what we're calling the "brain" is not just in our heads...the heart has an extensive network of nerves that process complex information and relay data upward to the brain in the skull....This data forms the foundation for visceral maps that help us have a "gut feeling" or a "heartfelt" sense." (Siegel, p. 43)

### Preparing to and doing it

*What is required of supervisors when working from the heart?*

A special kind of courage is required of those who work on the borderlands of the heart. If one opens one's heart to others, one is vulnerable, the experience of time changes, two resonate as one. In that territory, a person is seen with a clarity that only the heart can understand.

We live in super-rational times in which there is a general addiction to data (Friedman, 2007). With advances in science and technology, we are easily seduced into expecting immediate answers to even the most pressing and complex questions. We long for reassurance that all shall be well, often seeking that comfort in seemingly rational data that really isn't. Too often, leadership coaches attend to the external world of models, theories and actions without examining the internal world of their client. In Scharmer's Theory U, we are guided into a deeper exploration. He writes: "The nature of this inner place in leaders is something of a mystery."

Fundamentally, working with the heart requires acceptance of being a human among other humans. In *Born on the Continent – Ubuntu*, Getrude Matshe introduces the Zulu maxim, "umuntu ngumuntu ngabantu" or *Ubuntu* (Matshe, 2009). She explains:

A person is a person through other persons. The person with Ubuntu is open and available to others; and is affirming of others. A person with Ubuntu has the self-assurance that comes from knowing that they belong to a greater whole and are diminished when others are humiliated or diminished, when others are tortured, persecuted or oppressed. In other words, "I exist because you exist." (Matshe, 2009)

When we work from the heart, we are absolutely interdependent; the work does not exist in the supervisor or the supervisee – it exists in both.

This requires the supervisor to enter the work with humility, regardless of the amount of experience she or he has. Supervisors who prefer to mentor or guide from a position of superior knowledge will not enter this particular space.

**TIP**

Coaching supervision provides a practice field for seeing and being seen in a safe environment.

Working as a supervisor requires us to be sufficiently strong and vulnerable to truly open our hearts to resonance with our clients. In that place there is no hierarchy and we may even ask if there are one or two hearts at work. This is sacred ground filled with life-giving possibilities, myriad pitfalls and even seductions. Finally, it calls for the supervisor to be highly self-aware as well as self-forgiving and for all of us who coach to continue our own reflective practice in supervision.

### What does heart-to-heart work require of supervisees?

Edna Murdoch has often said, "Who you are is how you coach." As valuable as models and competencies are, they can remain like keys on the piano. Enormous amounts of practice and knowledge are required to apply them well, but even when the scales of music are understood and well rehearsed, it is the master pianist who makes brilliant music out of mechanical wires and wood. It is possible to review coaching cases from a tactical perspective and doing so is foundational for good coaching. Yet *someone* is doing the coaching and that someone can easily be hidden in technique. To take on coaching supervision is to venture into the coach him or herself.

**TIP**

It sometimes helps us to remember this simple axiom: 'Open heart before mouth." Or, following the advice of Thick Nat Hahn, "Breathing in I smile at you. Breathing out, I bring you peace." As an internal or external coach, try repeating this just before entering a client's office or calling on the telephone.

While we speak about the coach needing to be fully present when working with a client, heart-to-heart supervision requires just as much from the client or, in this case, the supervisee. In the case study of this chapter, the supervisee reports feeling terribly vulnerable – even exposed. As the work progressed, her willingness to be seen was the final ingredient needed to truly enter heart space. Going there is not a trivial decision for most people, and the supervisor must very gently provide a safe enough place for the supervisee to allow herself or himself to be seen. This is not a matter of technique so much as it is a stance, an intention and a very deeply held commitment to service.

**TIP**

Perhaps we are somehow drawn to certain supervisory relationships. In this case, there was the right chemistry from the beginning.

As you seek a supervisor, pay close attention to your own reaction to the person. Your heart will already know if there is a fit.

**CASE STUDY**

### Entering mystery by way of the heart

The case that follows is about the capacity and practice of entering this mysterious place by way of the heart and at the same time managing roles and boundaries. The story begins even before a supervision agreement because the roots of relationship begin there.

The supervisee, whom I call Sally for confidentiality, and I met 12 times. Sally is an exacting coach with many years of experience and a real dedication to serving her corporate clients. She offers coaching, training and consulting services to large enterprises. The work began with an exploration of Sally's most desirable mix of training, consulting and coaching and her feeling of being continually stressed. According to the

Full Spectrum Model, we focused on contracting and relationship building.

We will see that the very rational objectives Sally brought to the supervision, while valid, were not her core concerns. They may well have been addressed through coaching, but side references to other issues and the emotional content of her interaction with clients point to questions more suitable for supervision. Her comments suggested questions such as those offered by Otto Scharmer: Who is my Self? What is my work? (Scharmer, 2007)

As our relationship deepened, we found places of amazing co-presencing (Scharmer). Sally shared struggles with a teenage son. Using the Full Spectrum Model as a guide, we worked to distinguish coaching and counseling. We unpacked her experiences of clients, coaching contracts, the larger system the client lived in and the relationship between Sally and her clients. We experienced parallel processing and aspects of the same dance as occurred between Sally and her clients. Likewise, the dynamics of our relationship began to appear in her relationships with her clients. Parallel processing occurs in reverse as well.

There were moments of profound resonance between us in which images and learning emerged without effort. By working in that resonant space, we were able to explore the tension between situations when Sally played a strict professional role with her clients, which safe-guarded her vulnerability, and the moments of tremendous gifts to her clients when she allowed herself to be seen. As seen in the Full Spectrum Model, we were working with psychological perspectives.

## Opening hearts – the initial encounters

Sally and I met twice at professional meetings before agreeing to a supervisory contract. Consequently, our work began with some experience of each other in professional settings. Sally had the opportunity to experience how I think and work. We liked each other and found it enjoyable to converse. A relatively high assumption of trust was generated in these interactions that provided both a basis for successful supervision and the need to manage boundaries (Carroll, 2005).

## Progression toward heart-to-heart work

Early in our work together, Sally said that she wanted to develop criteria for saying 'no' more often to her clients as a way of reducing the stress in her life. Her question was not only for a specific client, but in general for her professional life. She has a tendency to accept enormous amounts of work and to then later become fatigued with the workload. Here, we touched into the Full Spectrum Model's attention to psychological perspective.

As I posed a series of questions about this pattern, Sally said that they were irritating her, but she said so with a smile and laugh. There was a certain playfulness that has carried through all of our work. Her ability to push back and for me to accept her response without withdrawing may also have built confidence – for both of us.

For a reason I cannot explain, I suddenly asked if I could share a story. It turns out she loves stories and metaphors, but I did not 'know' it at the time. I sensed that we were getting lost in question and answer exchanges without tapping more subtle information. One may say that I was rushing into depth, but by use of a story, we gently moved into a significant reflection (Lahad, 2000).

The spontaneous telling of the story offered an initial journey into Scharmer's U, beginning with "Open Mind".

Sally said she appreciated the story, but not for the same reasons I did. I attempted to focus on the moral of the story, which I had referenced in other situations. She ignored me and talked about parts that, for her, represented pollution, flexibility and play. This exchange seemed to make space for her, as if she claimed the right to have her own point of view. As we relaxed into our relationship, I believe she was beginning to move down Scharmer's U, toward the realm of Open Heart.

As time progressed, Sally persisted in driving herself and her clients very hard, and it became clear that some of this high-demand orientation appeared in how she evaluated her own work. Sally said that she rates her coaching sessions on a macro scale of excellent, good and OK, the latter meaning quite average – not great and not acceptable to her. I remarked that there was no bottom anchor to the scale and she responded, "If something is not working, I change it on the spot." My sense is that she has left little space for learning in the moment, or between sessions, and that she drives her clients as hard as she drives herself, perhaps to the point of mild narcissism (Murcoch, 2006) or perhaps she was expressing limited empathic listening (to her clients and herself), which requires an open heart (Scharmer).

*Wandering into emotions and a collective field*

In December, we began a series of sessions in which we seemed to wander. Sally was very tired and she was struggling with her teenage son. We explored the boundaries of our contract and relationship and easily agreed that her family concerns should be handled in other settings. However, co-creation of these limits offered a wonderful new question for me, "In the midst of all this, what do you want to work on?" And having asked this, a fog seemed to lift.

We both became present to our work, her professional work and our relationship in the moment.[1] As suggested in the Full Spectrum Model, we attended to boundary management.

## The heart-to-heart encounter

The next case she brought to a session was about her presence to a client's emotions. A human resource client was facing the loss of 60 positions. "She is afraid she is on the list, given her high salary and seniority." Something changed for Sally in that call, which she described as "not emotional but difficult". I had heard her talk about emotional situations while saying they were not emotional and wanted to press her on it. I asked what feelings she sensed in her client. Sally said, "We analyzed the situations, but not as feelings." I said, "How about you? What feelings did you sense in yourself?" She said, "I paced the client, respected her need to talk about it. I'm pretty empathetic, keeping an open heart connection – heart to heart – but not compassion – which is feeling sorry."

I felt myself react to this and suggested that empathy involves being able to identify the condition and feelings of the client and using that awareness for the benefit of the client.[2] Sally replied, "That definition seems dangerous. I have difficulty controlling emotions; I get moist eyes. I am moved, but I'm in control. I noticed my own reaction to something the client said and had real tears down my cheeks."

---

[1]  See Karyn Prentice on the effects of consciousness.

[2]  Learning in Action Technologies defines empathy in two ways. The first is "empathy accuracy" defined as the ability to "focus on the other and accurately identify what is going on (in) the other person, including what the other person is thinking, feeling, wanting and their intentions. It does not imply any feelings toward the other person. Empathy compassion means one is able to join the other person with compassion, knowing what it must be like to be them, including feeling the other's pain and joy. This includes the ability to stay connected with another person." (Johnson, 2007).

I, too, had tears in my eyes, and asked, "What's the difference between this moment we're experiencing and other moments?" Sally then offered this metaphor: "It's like developing fluid in the darkroom, as it slowly reveals an image (on paper)."

My reaction was in part the dichotomy I heard between keeping an open heart connection and the idea of not feeling compassion. To me they are inextricably linked.

I was very moved by her description of the darkroom and slow emergence of an image. My father was a photographer and taught me how to develop prints. I told her the effect of her comment (but not why I was sensitive to the metaphor) and described my own wet cheeks. Sally said, "But I'm not going to cry." I believed she was near tears and asked, "What moved you just now?" And she said, "That what I said moved you." We remained silent for a time and I experienced an intense moment of contact. It was very real and as if we were in the same room rather than 6,000 miles apart.

At that transformational, heart-to-heart moment, we sat in the sweet stillness of mutual authenticity and presence.

I found myself in "The container of transpersonal conversation".[3] Erik de Haan describes the importance of this encounter: "The heightened emotion of the 'here and now' of the coaching relationship at the point when a critical moment arises seems to be important for facilitating the learning of the coachee. We can argue therefore, that learning through coaching is as much an emotional process as a cognitive process" (de Haan, 2008). "When the coaching relationship is able to 'contain' these heightened emotions, then the moment can be reflected upon by coach and coachee, raising the possibility for the coachee to explore new options, both in this relationship, in other relationships generally, and in the work place"

---

[3] See chapter by Karyn Prentice.

(de Haan, 2008). In the partnership of supervision it is essential that both members are able to stay in that emotional moment. If they are, they are practicing transformation through a heart-to-heart encounter.

Why not simply call it *love*, especially in the sense described by CS Lewis as "agape" (Lewis, 1958)? It is not a loving of someone or something; it is not a temporal or erotic love. Lewis says agape is love itself, which is completely dissociated from any need or want, a fullness that gives away.

Sally wrote after this encounter, "Thank you again for our last conversation which brought me so much insight – I could sense a true connection at the end, at the moment when I was deeply in touch with my own emotions – there was a sense of mutual and deep human resonance" (private email correspondence, 2009). The experience we shared in a few heartbeats shaped everything that came later and, eventually, shaped moments between Sally and a client.

I found myself feeling very close to my supervisee and quite exposed. Frankly, I noticed an erotic tension in me and began asking myself if I had sufficient boundaries to work this close to a female client without violating the sacredness of the situation and the relationship. My concern reflected the Full Spectrum Model's systemic awareness and ethics. To resolve this tension, I asked, "How could you use this great capability of yours to connect heart to heart more fully in coaching?" Her answer encompassed her life far beyond this client: "It's very helpful, reminding me of working more in the center. It is also revealing about my son." I added, "And trusting yourself," which was as much to me as it was to her. "What are you feeling now?" I asked. She said, "Softness, humility, acceptance... weakness."

The effect of staying in the moment in service of the supervisee rippled into the coach's own experience both in the here and now and to the larger field including her son, who is not directly part of our work. It also paralleled her meeting with her clients – her initial resistance to emotions, then opening her heart and being present to her humanity and that of her client. How sad it is, however, that we so often associate softness, humility and acceptance with weakness.

## Open heart before mouth

A very easy way to move toward the heart is to say to yourself before, during or after a supervision session, "I open my heart to this person before opening my mouth."

As simple as it sounds, just saying these words allows you to connect at a more profound heart level any time you feel that your heart is closing, or you are reacting negatively to another person.

At the Coaching Supervision Academy, we are strong advocates for extensive training or formation before offering coaching supervision. During practice, observation by others and feedback, we learn to notice subtle sensations in ourselves and to make in-the-moment decisions about how to use them. Supervision training provides a practice field for developing this precision.

## Consequences of working heart to heart

Shifts were happening in the entire field. Each time Sally made a shift in her relationship with her client, she reported a shift in the situation with her son – a sort of non-local benefit from our work (Mansfield, 1996). As she reported moving to a role of parent–coach with her son, she was also reducing her driven attitude toward her clients. She worked more on their goals and less on hers. She began to arrive in supervision sessions just as she was – a person, a concerned mother, an accomplished coach – and we created a holding environment for her humanity and a practice field for managing the boundaries and balance of work and personal life – which had been an initial objective in seeking supervision.

## What is required of supervisors?

What special attention may be required for this kind of work? We believe that silence is the most basic requirement, for we are entering into soul territory. At this level of communication, words are easily a distraction. This is sacred ground, a place set apart from normal time and place. Deep respect is needed as well, which suggests "the supervisor 'tunes in' to their coach/client's field whilst keeping their own 'stuff' out of the equation" (Orriss, 2005).

Courage is also required. In 2003, while watching lava from Hawaii's Kilauea volcano pour into the sea, I pictured how the creation of something new has a certain violence to it. Red liquid rock fell into the water and boiled the edges of the Pacific Ocean. A bit of earth was born. The poem I wrote later ended with these lines: "Knowing now what violence it took for God to make the world in only 7 days, I resist my own creation" (Magill, 2006: 88-89). In transformational learning, there is destruction; the false self, the denying of heart self, the protecting self are destroyed for the moment. At the very same time, the open hearted work allows the birth of a truer self, one more authentic and more able to dwell with other human beings.

## Try this –

*Before walking in the door*

Whether you are physically entering a building to meet with a supervisee, starting a Skype conversation or picking up the telephone, stop for a moment. Breathe gently and deeply. Then picture the person you are about to meet. Welcome the coming encounter. See the deep humanity of the other person – and your own. If you truly welcome this person and the relationship, you will almost certainly feel a smile on your face and in your heart. Now enter and join with the person you have come to meet. You are ready for heart-centered supervision.

## Ways to begin

If that is new territory, the exercises offered by HeartMath provide a safe entry point.

When we are ready to join our clients/supervisees in the depth of a heart-to-heart connection, we may ask questions like these:

1. What else is going on in and around me that may distract me?

2. What can I do with those things for the next while if I want to help now?

3. What motives do I have for wanting to work heart to heart?

4. What boundary and what openness are appropriate in separating the coming encounter from the last one?

5. Given all that, am I willing to engage in heart-to-work work?

If the answer to the last question is yes, it is time to reflect on what we know about the supervisee.

1. What do we know about this person's readiness for this work?

2. What factors in our contract and in our relationship provide the permission to work in this intimate space?

3. What does the supervisee want in the here and now?

> Frankly, there's a risk in asking all these questions. They are good in theory, but if we had stopped to answer them in that heart-to-heart moment, it would have been our heads that answered. Our intelligent hearts didn't need to analyze.

The flip sides of these questions are for the supervisee to answer.

**1.** Today, now, what do I want from the next few minutes?

**2.** What thoughts and feelings do I have about my coaching supervisor?

**3.** What happened last time we met that worked well for me?

**4.** What happened that troubles me a bit?

**5.** What am I looking for that I am willing to be fully present, fully open to this conversation?

**6.** If I have reservations, am I able to bring them to my supervisor now?

## Additional tips for working together
**– adapted from Edgar Schein in *Helping* (Schein, 2009)**

**1.** Confirm the presence of an equitable relationship. This is not a time for inflated egos on any side. Are both people ready, willing and able to work this way? Has the supervisee kept his or her own voice and authority?

**2.** Be prepared to do nothing. This is a very unique sort of journey with much more attention to being than to action. It is well described in the Taoist notion of Wei Wu Wei – Action without effort or Do without doing. The most powerful moment of the case study occurred in the photographic darkroom metaphor. First there was an image we could both hold; insight occurred effortlessly.

**3.** While supervisor and supervisee co-create the moment and both benefit/learn/grow/heal in the process, the ownership of the reflection and insight rests with the supervisee. Certainly, the supervisor will also have learned, but that probably does not belong in the conversation. The supervisor may sense time to move apart, to rebound, to become more distinct… to ask questions from a witness place more than a co-creator place. The supervisor bears responsibility for holding the outer container of the experience and for boundary management.

## Try this:

To work from our hearts, we must be clear about our intentions. There are schools of thought in coaching that the coach drives the client toward the client's stated objectives. Similarly, some forms of supervision are aimed at evaluation and feedback on coaching skills. But here, we are talking about the fine tuning of the instrument, the coach. Check-in often, asking, "What are my intentions right now?"

## Work with delicate intention

In her exhaustive reporting on the power of intention, Lynne McTaggert reports the experiences of healers working through intention.

> *"I had assumed that intention was like a strong 'oomph,' or mental push, through which you project your thoughts to another person to ensure that your wishes were carried out. But the healers [I studied] described a very different process: intention requires initial focus, but then a type of surrender, a letting go of the self as well as the outcome.*

**McTaggart, 2007: 81**

Paradoxically, while we have a clear desire to serve and we want concrete outcomes of effective coaching or learning, we must let it all go to work from the heart. The Full Spectrum Model calls us to self-awareness and support.

Working from the heart is then:

**Intentional** – with the intent being one of opening ourselves not as wise solution givers but more as witnesses being present on behalf of the other.

**Joint** – while one may open alone, the powerful transformational work occurs when supervisor and supervisee join in the effort.

**Aware** – listening at a very deep level. As images emerge, we step back and let them arrive.

## Boundary management

In supervision we must hold our boundaries and authority (Hawkins, 2006: 144). It is not enough to be *only* open to our humanity or to *only* hold authority. We must have the courage and dexterity to dance between our hearts and our minds, between our role and our humanity and between us as separate and connected people.

We are not copies of one another and our distinctions plus our connections allow for reflection and learning. Sallyé Linden writes:

> By separate, I do not mean to sever, to block off, to isolate, or become detached but rather to make a distinction. Connected is to be linked, to have a relationship. How can you have a relationship or be linked to someone or something if you are not separate? If there is no distinction, between you and the other, who is making the connection?
>
> (Linden, 2008: 3-4)

## Important boundaries

**BOUNDARY 1: ego and fear.** If a supervisor fears his own competency or is uncomfortable with a supervisee, he will be guarded. For when one is open, one is seen. It is as if we open the door to our carefully guarded house and invite the community of supervisees to look in. How exposing it would be. What if the supervisee discovers we have the same fears as he or she does? What if the supervisee discovers we have made mistakes in our coaching? I must maintain distinctions between my thoughts and feelings about me and my thoughts and feelings about being in this specific moment.

**BOUNDARY 2: needs.** We can't pretend that we don't have needs. They cross our mind and, if we have a good boundary, we nod to them and consider what place they have. If they don't make a contribution in the moment, we must set them aside to be met later. The supervisee's need in the moment and our need in the moment are distinct from each other.

**BOUNDARY 3: time management.** Spaciousness in coaching supervision is an antidote to the busy lives of coaches and their clients. While the timelessness of heart-to-heart work is very real, the clock is also ticking. It is the supervisor's job to manage both. Poor time boundaries mess up schedules and may be a way of lessoning the intensity of critical moments.

**BOUNDARY 4: learning.** The learning derived during supervision is important to both supervisor and supervisee, but in the tender space of this work, we must make sure that we don't impose our learning on the supervisee. Sometimes we can share our discoveries; at other times we must keep them to ourselves.

**BOUNDARY 5: feelings.** Although we can share many feelings with our supervisees, we must sort out on the fly which of the feelings we are experiencing are valid for sharing in service of the supervisee. The experience of love that we may have is just ours. We may hold the image of our supervisee with love, but we probably cannot say in that moment, "I love you."

**BOUNDARY 6: vulnerability.** To what extent are we comfortable with what is arriving in the heart-to-heart space? If we can't handle our own anxiety, we can't do the work. If we avoid being vulnerable, we won't let go of our need to control as a means of being safe.

**BOUNDARY 7: doing our own work.** Our work as supervisors clearly has the potential to alter both ourselves and our supervisees in substantial ways we scarcely understand. While the benefit is great, there is also the potential for misuse of such connections. If we are to work in this territory, we are well advised to continue receiving our own supervision.

## Transformational learning

What exactly do we mean by 'transformational learning' and what happens to us when it happens? It strikes me that we use the expression far too casually in business, coaching and life generally.

Perhaps overused but still instructive, the analogy of the caterpillar transforming into a butterfly suggests an irreversible change. That's fine and well for bugs, but what do we really mean when it comes to human beings?

One source for answering this question comes from the world of poetry and of the poets who write the poems. Contemporary American poet, Mark Nepo, has been enormously influenced by the changes he has faced in his long and life-threatening struggle with cancer. His poetry has been widely embraced in the health care community as a guide to the deep experience of that difficult journey. In the introduction to Nepo's 2007 book entitled, *Surviving Has Made Me Crazy*, Dr Rich Frankel reminds us that what we call 'health' is a state of homeostasis – a constantly adjusting effort to keep things as they are. Frankel writes: "[Nepo's] experience of surviving a life threatening disease is not a return to homeostasis, the way things were, but rather a radical transformation from which there is no turning back" (Frankel cited in Nepo, 2007).

The heart-to-heart moments of coaching supervision and of other contexts as well, are truly changes of form: form, not in the physical sense, but in our understanding of ourselves and others. In my poem, "The Voice of God", I wrote of such an encounter:

> *The moment full contact with others comes,*
> *We can never go back to being separate.*
> *When the many become one song,*
> *We are touched by our one human heart and*
> *There is no recovery.*

**Magill, 2006**

So transformational learning – through reflective practice – may teach us that a) we are not alone, b) we are each part of the overall human experience, c) like it or not we are in this together and d) being open hearted with another person allows insight that direct conversation would muddy. Sally, in the case study, had said that compassion was dangerous and moved to allow herself to feel her feelings, to be more compassionate with her clients and to help her clients do the same. Going back to the way things were would be very difficult.

In the end, working heart to heart is both a choice and a discipline. Our perspective is that everyone has the capacity to do so, but not everyone takes on the discipline. If one accepts, even tentatively, the benefit of working heart to heart, why doesn't everyone?

Perhaps there are two key reasons. First, the fear of being exposed. Second, the fear of doing harm. If a client knows we have our own flaws, will he or she still respect us? Will we be worthy of being paid for this work? Will we be embarrassed? Will we, now that we know we are imperfect, harm the client? Erik de Haan describes three categories of critical moments in coaching, hence also in supervision of coaching. To paraphrase de Haan, there are critical moments of method, of relationship and of existence (de Haan, 2008). The latter of these seems most relevant to working heart to heart, because our self-image is at stake.

If these fears prevent us from transformational work in coaching, we will benefit from participating in supervision. If they are intractable, we may benefit from deeper therapy before continuing.

At the end we must ask, "So what?" With all the potential traps and vulnerabilities of such intimate work, why would one enter this heart space? The answer is very simple: Transformational learning requires us to be changed, and to be changed we must allow ourselves to be seen and experienced. If we withdraw at the critical moment of transparency so vital to great learning, we cheat ourselves and our clients.

The physical heart opens and closes to do its job of pumping blood. Supervising heart to heart is no different.

## REFERENCES

**Carroll, M and Gilbert, Maria C (2005)** On Being a Supervisee: Creating learning partnerships, London, UK: Vukani Publishing.

**De Haan, E (2008)** Relational Coaching, Chichester, UK: John Wiley & Son Ltd.

**Friedman, E (2007)** A Failure of Nerve: Leadership in the age of the quick fix, New York, US: Church Publishing.

**Hawkins, P and Smith, N (2006)** Coaching, Mentoring and Organizational Consultancy: Supervision and development, London, UK: Open University Press.

**Johnson, J (2007)** EQ in Action Profile: Certification training manual, Bellevue, Washington, US: Learning In Action Technologies.

**Lahad, M (2000)** Creative Supervision: The use of expressive arts methods in supervision and self-supervision, London, UK: Jessica Kingsley.

**Lewis, C (1958)** The C.S. Lewis Recordings: The four loves, New York, US: Episcopal Radio-TV Foundation.

**Linden, S (2008)** Boundaries and human relationships, Carmarthen, UK: Crown House Publishing Ltd.

**McTaggart, L (2007)** The Intention Experiment, New York, US: Free Press.

**Magill, SP (2006)** Fully Human: A book of verse, Edmonds, Washington, US: Balcladdoch Press.

**Magill, S P (2009, September 26)** Interview with Gertrude Matshe.

**Mansfield, V and Spiegelman, J M (1996)** On the physics and psychology of the transference as an interactive field, Published in: Journal of Analytical Psychology, 1996 pp 11-16, US.

**Matshe, G (2009).** Born on the Continent – Ubuntu, Christ Church, Oxford, UK: Getrude Matshe.

**Murcoch, E (2006)** Recognizing and working with the narcissistic personality, Coaching Supervision Academy Ltd. [Unpublished article]

**Nepo, M (2007)** Surviving Has Made Me Crazy, Fort Lee, New Jersey, US: CavanKerry Press Ltd.

**Orriss, M (2005)** The Working Alliance, Coaching Supervision Academy Ltd. [Unpublished article]

**Schein, E (2009)** Helping, San Francisco, US: Berrett-Koehler Publishers Inc.

**Seigel, Daniel J (2011)** Mindsight: The new science of personal transformation, New York, US: Bantam Books.

## FURTHER READING

**Lewis, TA (2000)** A General Theory of Love, New York, US: Random House.

# 4 | *Reflective learning and the reflective practitioner*

- Elaine Patterson

## Abstract

IN THIS chapter you will discover that reflective learning sits at the heart of coaching supervision and the Full Spectrum Model.

The power of reflective learning lies in our ability to inquire and learn from our experiences. The core purpose of coaching supervision is to facilitate the development of our clients' reflective learning practices in order to become reflective practitioners.

These processes can be joyful and fun, illuminating blind spots and encouraging us to be our best selves. But they can also be challenging, embarrassing or distressing as we hold the mirror up to ourselves. This requires coach supervisors to create safe open spaces where our clients discover their own courage and compassion to inquire deeply into their own experiences, make meaning and apply their learning.

The chapter will therefore offer a working definition of reflective learning and reflective practice and what this means for coaching supervision. It will also explore why this has become increasingly important now and will share tools, models and techniques to help coaching supervisors create safe open spaces for the development of their clients as reflective practitioners. The chapter will also introduce a new model for reflective learning to complement the Full Spectrum Model. The chapter will be brought alive with Top Tips and exercises. At the end, two Coach supervisors share their experiences of reflective learning.

## Introduction

This chapter will de-bunk the myth that reflective learning is tedious and it will put it center stage in coaching supervision profession. Reflective learning empowers us to see our experience with fresh eyes, open hearts and freed minds. Reflective learning practices enable us to stay connected, alive and awake to all of what we are doing and how we are being as coaches and coaching supervisors as we work with our clients.

However, reflective learning is often seen as the poor relation in the literature. This is because it is probably the hardest of the different learning styles to grasp and apply in our busy, frenetic world. The challenge to the coaching and coaching supervision professions is to give reflective practice the space, recognition and investment it deserves as our core competency that helps to unlock the latent potential in individuals, teams and organizations.

Reflective learning also holds the Coaching Supervision Academy's Full Spectrum Model together. This is because reflective practice is the invisible thread and the core generic competency that gives coaching supervisors the tools to help us help others learn how they learn and to then learn, unlearn and relearn as we encounter new experiences, insights and learning. Work in one of the perspectives of the Full Spectrum Model energetically feeds and nourishes all of the other perspectives within the model.

## Towards A working definition of reflective learning and reflective practice

What then do we mean by 'reflective learning' and 'reflective learning practices'?

Fortunately, history and philosophy tells us that there is nothing new in our need as human beings to reflect – in our love of storytelling, in our search for meaning – and in people's need to create space, place and time for contemplation, meditation and reflection. As Socrates said:

> *"The unexamined life is not worth living for a human being."*

**Socrates, between 470 BC and 399 BC**

A survey of the literature shows a confusing array of definitions for 'reflective learning' and 'reflective practice'. The actual word 'reflection' stems from the Latin meaning 'to bend back, to stand apart from, to stand outside of'.

For the purposes of this chapter 'reflective learning' is defined as:

> *"the active process of witnessing, inquiring and exploring into our own experience(s) in order to examine that experience and to create the possibility of learning from that experience."*

**adapted from Amulya, 2008**

The key to effective reflective learning is learning how to openly, honestly, compassionately and courageously inquire, examine, review, question, re-evaluate and own our experiences (our own feelings, thoughts, assumptions, behavior and actions within a situation) in order to learn, to reframe *and* to learn how to apply that learning going forward. Learning is thus emergent and is constructed through a dialog with self, with others, and interaction with the world.

A reflective learning practice is a regular habit, structure or routine that is applied to the processes of reflective learning.

A reflective learning practitioner is therefore a practitioner who consciously and intentionally applies and lives reflective learning practices to his or her professional practice. It becomes a way of being in the world.

Distinctions are often made in the literature between 'reflection' and 'critical reflection'. For the purposes of this chapter the difference lies in the depth of inquiry and challenge that the learner engages in with the material of his or her experience. For the purposes of this chapter reflection is understood to focus more on the 'how' and 'how to' whereas critical reflection challenges the 'why' of what we are doing and how we are being. Mezirow (1990) helpfully described this as differentiating between the content and the process of reflection and examining basic premises that were informing an issue or dilemma. Critical reflection is achieved when practitioners are able to challenge their frames of reference with their underlying beliefs, assumptions and consequences. It is in this way that critical reflective learning makes transformational learning possible.

## Why is this important?

Reflective practice exploded on to the stage with Schon's publication of *The Reflective Practitioner: How professionals think in action* in 1983. This built on earlier writing and research from such key influencers as John Dewey, Kurt Lewin, Chris Argyris, Jean Piaget and Carl Jung who were all exploring the inter-relationships, experience, reflection, learning, growth and development.

But what Schon (1983) did was to explicitly state the limits of technical training that served as essentially the bare minimum to secure entry into the professions. Schon argued that this training did not necessarily equip practitioners with the processes to handle the many gray areas of professional practice where problems were messy and complex and where they often brought us face to face with our own humanity and the humanity of others.

As Schon wrote:

> *In the varied topography of professional practice there is a high hard ground overlooking the swamp. On the high ground manageable problems lend themselves to solution through the application of research-based theory & technique. The irony of this situation is that the problems of the high ground tend to be relatively unimportant to individuals and to society at large, however great their technical interest may be, while in the swamp lie the problems of greatest human concern. The practitioner must choose. Shall he/she remain on the high ground where he/she can solve relatively unimportant problems according to prevailing standards or rigour or shall he/she descend into the swamp of important problems and non rigorous inquiry?* - **Schon ,1983: 42**

Coaching supervision exists to serve in the messy swamps of practice where we come up against gray areas of ethics, morals, values and all aspects of the human condition. This is where day-to-day pressures can erode what is important and can compromise integrity through the disconnect between what we believe and value and what we actually do.

The disconnects are often the spaces between what we aspire to do and how we are actually being. Schon (1983) described this as the difference between "espoused action" and "theory–in-action". Johns (2008) described this as working with the difference between the vision and actual practice so that vision comes closer to a lived reality. These gaps are often first noticed as a sense of unease or discomfort that is signaling some possible contradiction, ambiguity or paradox within the supervisee's work.

Typical stories that are brought to supervision by supervisees can include, for example: a deep reaction that has been evoked in the coach by a client that is preventing the coach from working without bias or judgment; conflicts of interest within the supervisory relationship; appropriate disclosure of information or material; coaches unconsciously colluding with the wider systemic energies at work; coaches unable to resist the temptation to strategize and going into fix-it mode for their clients; or the possible identification of dubious practices.

Reflective learning is often seen as the most challenging of the four stages in, for example, Kolb's Learning Cycle (1984). The four stages are: Concrete Experience; Reflective Observation; Abstract Conceptualization; and Active Experimentation. Countless leaders, coaches and coach supervisors in training regularly complain of the challenges they face in engaging with reflective learning, preferring to shortcut or indeed avoid the stage of reflective observation. Understanding this is central to the coaching supervisor's ability to be a learning facilitator. This will be explored further later in the chapter.

**TIP**

Spot potential disconnections by being alert to:

▼   *possible contradictions*

▼   *unresolved dilemmas*

▼   *unanswered questions*

▼   *dilemmas*

▼   *lack of authenticity*

**Try this**

Why do you think that people are likely to find reflective learning difficult or uncomfortable?

Likely reasons: ...

**How does the coach supervisor help supervisees to learn how to learn reflectively?**

▼   *This new focus invites us to consider what then needs to be in the coaching supervisor's toolkit to help their supervisees learn how to learn reflectively.*

**TIP**

A common error is to often mistake reflection and reflective learning as just thinking about something *but* what we mean within the context of the supervisory relationship is reflection for the purpose of learning. Reflective learning is focused on helping supervisees learn deeply from their experiences. It is about helping supervisees to become alive to their experiences, to raise their awareness, to awaken, to question, to challenge, to shift perspectives, to reframe and to see with fresh eyes.

## Starting points

The coach supervisor needs to join his or her supervisees with where they are in their sense and understanding of what is meant by 'reflective learning' and what practices they have already developed.

The following exercise helps both you and your supervisee understand their point along their journey.

**TIP**

To create the optimum conditions for reflective learning:

▼ *deep breathing*

▼ *any form of meditation, e.g. sitting or walking*

▼ *focusing on a beautiful object, e.g. an art work or a flower*

▼ *visualization*

▼ *memories of happy times or something that inspired you*

▼ *a quotation or a poem*

▼ *a piece of music*

## Try this

Self-assessment: What is my starting point?

**1.** What do I understand by 'reflection' and 'reflective learning'?

**2.** How reflective am I? How can I evidence that?

**3.** How important is developing a reflective learning practice to me, both personally and professionally?

*Preparation*

Reflective learning requires us to access all aspects of our intelligences, personality and inner wisdom. This means that both the coach supervisor and the supervisee need to design their own processes or rituals to switch off from the noise of the 'to do list'.

Both supervisor and supervisee are encouraged to create their own inner and outer conditions for reflective learning. None of this needs to be complicated but will be different for each of us. Top Tips and suggestions are given in the box. Optimum states or conditions that enable the supervisee to learn reflectively include stillness, openness, curiosity, courage and compassion.

Such steps help both the supervisor and the supervisees to start to retreat from our left brain, logical, rational, judgmental thinking processes and open us up to experience – to experience experience. This is critical as reflective learning requires us to be present to ourselves so that we can question our frames of reference and be able to reconnect with our innate wisdom and inner knowing.

*Role and qualities of the coach supervisor*

The Coach supervisor is responsible for creating and holding a safe, reflective learning space for the supervisee to bring his or her issues. This starts with contracting but must be nurtured moment by moment in the session and over the course of the supervisory relationship.

The role of the coaching supervisor is to act as the wise, compassionate observer and as witness, providing support and challenge and using what he or she is noticing and all of who he or she is to facilitate the supervisees' reflective learning – unfreezing blocks and obstacles to the free flow of learning. A self-assessment exercise around these core competencies follows.

## Try this

*Self-assessment coaching supervisor's meta-qualities for creating a reflective learning environment*

### Rate 0-5 (0 is poor; 5 is excellent)

▼ *Mindful presence*
▼ *Finding stillness, space and spaciousness*
▼ *Quality of attention and intention*

▼ *Appreciation and generosity*

▼ *Curiosity*

▼ *Respect*

▼ *Compassion*

▼ *Authenticity*

▼ *Spontaneity*

▼ *Openness*

▼ *Acceptance.*

*Structuring a coaching supervision session*

The following exercise offers some structure to support the contracting and running of a coaching supervision session to help to create the optimum environment for reflective learning. This is central as coaching supervision works in and through the relationship and in the conversation.

Essentially, we learn through the stories of our experiences. An experience may be an event, an action, a thought, a feeling, a worry, an impression, an unease, a conversation, an article or an observation and a set of simple questions posed in the spirit of curiosity and non-judgmental appreciative inquiry are all that is needed to get started.

### Try this

*Shaping a session*

▼ *Welcoming and connecting: extending a gesture of presence toward each other (for example, a moment of silence; a pause before starting the work; or some shared meditation together).*

▼ *Extending an invitation: for example, asking, "How would you like to use our time together?" or "What do you want to look at today?" or "What is your question?"*

▼ *Clarifying intention: for example, asking, "And what would you like by the end of the session?"*

▼ *Ensuring what will best serve: for example, asking, "How do you want me to be with you?"*

Then the body of the work:

▼ *Closure: for example by focusing on the learning points by asking, "And so what have you learned today?"*

▼ *Disconnecting: by honoring the work and closing down the session.*

Within the body of the work simple reflective questions as shown in Top Tips can be all that is needed.

Many models have been developed for facilitating reflection – for example, Boyd and Fales' "Stages of Reflection (1983)", Gibbs' "Reflective Cycle (1988)" and Johns' "Model of Structured Reflection (14th edition) (2004)". The variety of models can be confusing but at the heart of all of these models sits a series of simple (but not necessarily easy) questions for inquiry.

The Coaching Supervision Academy's Full Spectrum Model alerts us to a 360 inquiry into all aspects of our practice that we may need to pay attention to and bring to supervision. But the key is not in slavishly following a linear set of questions but in the spirit of openness and creativity by which we approach and use our experiences to help us to learn, develop, grow and find meaning… helping our clients to become all of who they are.

**TIP**

Simple reflective questions

**1.** What was happening? What did you notice?

**2.** What were you thinking and feeling? How were you behaving during the experience?

**3.** What are the main learning points for you from the experience?

**4.** How is your learning going to be applied in the future? What may you do differently?

**adapted from The OCM Reflection Note Template**

The following exercise invites you to consider the extent to which coaching supervisors are creating the favorable conditions for reflective learning.

## Try this

*Self-assessment favorable conditions*

*Self-assessment*

### 0–5 (0 is poor; 5 is excellent)

- ▼ *building a strong learning partnership or working alliance*
- ▼ *contracting for safety, trust, permissions, support, challenge, honesty and feedback*
- ▼ *providing safe space, structures and processes*
- ▼ *testing the supervisee's readiness and motivations for his or her own learning and change*
- ▼ *holding the supervisee as resourceful, responsible and accountable*
- ▼ *flexing style to meet the particular context and the supervisee's own preferences and style in order to access their multiple intelligences*
- ▼ *acting as the facilitator to the learning process of others – that is, as a witness and as a wise, compassionate observer*
- ▼ *honoring and celebrating successes.*

*Different formats for reflective learning*

Reflective learning can take place in a number and range of different contexts. These include:

- ▼ *reflecting alone*
- ▼ *1:1 supervision sessions*
- ▼ *group supervision sessions*
- ▼ *action learning sets*

▼ *mentoring*

▼ *at the end of team meetings to review learning.*

Reflective learning is both a solitary and a social activity. Complete the following exercise to discover the best mix for you.

**Try this**

Finding the right mix for me. A range of different practices can help to embed the practice of reflective learning. These include:

▼ *writing a Journal*

▼ *writing up structured reflection notes*

▼ *making time for regular pauses in the busy day-today schedule to take stock*

▼ *reflecting in the moment as the situation unfolds*

▼ *developing a regular meditation or reflection time slot during the day or over the week.*

*Deeper insights into the world of reflective learning*

This section goes on to briefly outline some key theories and concepts that can help the coaching supervisor facilitate reflective learning and practice. The field is huge and this is not an exhaustive list or a complete review of all that is currently available.

These are:

▼ *understanding the difference between reflection in action and reflection on action*

▼ *understanding the difference between espoused theory and theory in action*

▼ *understanding the processes of learning*

▼ *understanding our different types of knowing, learning and adult development*

▼ *understanding adult learners' needs for trust and safety*

▼ *understanding the blocks to learning and change.*

*Understanding the difference between reflection in action and reflection on action*

Schon (1983) coined the phases "reflection in action" and "reflection on action" to distinguish between two different types of reflection that occur at different times. The analogy of dance floor and balcony helps to differentiate between the two.

"Reflection in action" occurs when we are in the *midst* of an experience – when we are on the dance floor. This means that we are able to pause and be present to all that we are experiencing *and we are able to examine* what we are thinking, feeling and how we are behaving as the experience unfolds.

"Reflection on action" is reflection *after* the experience – standing above from the balcony – in order to gain new insights and learning in order to inform future practice. This helps us to make explicit the implicit and what is needing to emerge.

Some texts also describe a third position that is reflection for action. This is reflective learning *after* the experience, which helps us to anticipate future scenarios and try to plan our reactions and choices accordingly.

A variation on Johari's Window (Luft and Ingham 1950) (see Figure 4.1) provides a helpful framework where reflection is helping us to identify our blind spots – waking us to up to what we cannot see, shifting from subject to object. This is the area of potential development in the supervisory relationship.

## Subject to Object - **The Johari Window**

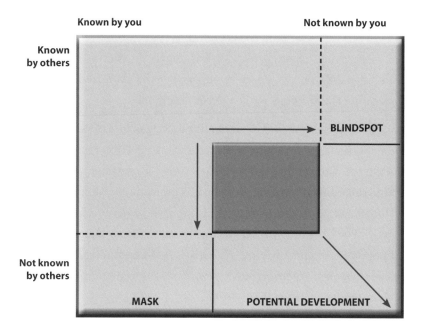

© Liz Buckle and Elaine Paterson

**Figure 4.1 -** *Johari Window*

*Understanding the difference between espoused theory and theory in action*

Schon (1983) coined the phrases "reflection in action" and "reflection on action" to distinguish between two different types of reflection that occur at different times. The analogy of dance floor and balcony helps to differentiate between the two.

Reflective learning practices can help enable the practitioner to work toward becoming as close as is possible to his or her best self and what best serves his or her clients.

*Understanding the processes of learning*

Understanding the learning style and the learning cycle is a way of sharing a common language in supervision.

Converting experiences into learning is a process, and there are huge differences between a supervisee who 'does reflection' to 'becoming' and 'being' a reflective practitioner.

Kolb (1984) helpfully described four stages in Kolb's Learning Cycle. These are: Concrete Experience, Reflective Observation, Abstract Conceptualization, and Active Experimentation. All four stages need to be experienced in order to optimize learning. Honey and Mumford mapped learning style preferences on to the cycle. Four learning styles were identified. These were Activist, Pragmatist, Reflector and Theorist. Self-assessments to help readers identify their preferred styles and associated development plans are available via their website.

The DIKW (data, information, knowledge and wisdom) Hierarchy (Rowley, 2007) offers a way of understanding the journey that can (but does not necessarily) occur through a reflective learning process when data or experiences are converted into information that can then be converted into knowledge and that is then converted into practical wisdom. Central for the supervisor in helping the supervisee's reflective learning is to unlock the emotion behind the need for the learning, however, helping the practitioner to shift from the 'knowing what' of practice through to 'knowing how' to 'knowing why' to – crucially – 'caring why'.

Complementing these is the work of Otto Scharmer's Theory U (2008), which is concerned with helping the supervisor and the supervisee to track the conversation. This can help both to locate where they are within their session, mapping the depth of inquiry and discovery that is occurring.

As shown below, Scharmer describes the learning process as a "U", where it is possible for us to learn to shift our inner attention from habitual downloading (at the top left-hand corner of the U) to a state of presencing (at the bottom of the U), which then creates new possibilities and solutions (emerging at the top right hand of the U) in seven distinct movements.

These are from stopping, suspending and really observing and starting to listen; to noticing and seeing with fresh eyes and with an open mind; to sensing the whole from our hearts; to retreating and reflecting connecting to a wider essential truth or source – a letting go in order to let come – to reframe, sense new possibilities and act in an instant from the emerging whole; to formulating; to experimenting; and to performing. They are shown (see Figure 4.2) and outlined below.

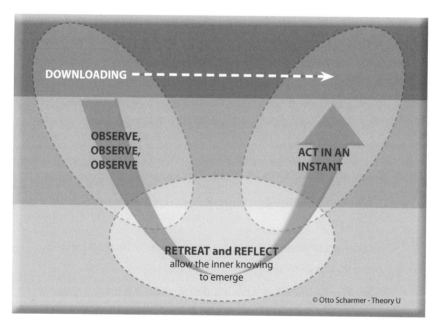

**Figure 4.2** - *Learning from the future as it emerges*
*(adapted from Scharmer's (2007) Theory U)*

This process can also help the practitioner shift from apprentice to master; from linear to intuitive thinking; from subject to object; from seeing the parts to seeing the whole; from fragmentation to holistic; from reliance on external to internal points of reference and authority; and from seeing self as separate to self as "we" and part of the bigger system at work. This connects with the much wider world of universal energy fields, quantum consciousness and systems thinking is the subject of other chapters in this book.

*Understanding the different levels of knowing, learning and adult development*

To "know" is to "identify and recognize a thing, person or place", which is different from knowledge, which is a "practical or theoretical understanding of a thing, person or fact" (OED, 1975). However, important research by Belenky, Clinchy, Goldberger, and Tarule (1986) that examined women's ways of knowing has shown that there are five different perspectives to people's levels of knowing. Identifying which of these five perspectives the supervisee is working at can help to indicate his or her stage of development and identify how the coaching supervisor can support his or her supervisees to become free, independent and reflective practitioners.

These five perspectives are:

1. silence where the practitioner does not have his or her own voice
2. received knowing where the practitioner listens and speaks the voices of others
3. subjective knowing where the practitioner is listening to his or her own inner voice
4. procedural knowing where the practitioner is able to listen and speak both from a place of connected empathetic

knowing and a place of separate rational and logical knowing (often characterized as the feminine and masculine ways of knowing)

5. constructed knowing where the practitioner is able to weave together and integrate subjective and procedural knowing into a compassionate, wise and assertive voice. As Johns writes (2004: 11): "[F]rom the perspective of the constructed voice practitioners view all knowledge as contextual, experience themselves as creators of knowledge and value both subjective and objective strategies for knowing."

Carroll (2005) described a similar approach in what he called "Five Levels of Reflection". These are:

**Level 1:** where the reflection focuses on self "me" – the practitioner – alone

**Level 2:** where reflection focuses on self "me" either/or thinking and my immediate relationships

**Level 3:** where reflection starts to explore authenticity, looking beyond the immediate experience to principles

**Level 4:** where reflection starts to connect across themes or categories searching for the principles by which we give meaning

**Level 5:** where reflection embraces difference and diversity.

This research also reads across to the work of Bloom *et al.* (1953). Bloom *et al.* researched the different levels or taxonomy of learning. This essentially described the extent to which learners engaged with their learning and the different outcomes for learning along a continuum that stretches from passive to critical engagement with the experience to reframing, meaning making and integration of the learning from the experience.

Senge (2004) helpfully identified that there were three levels or loops of learning, building on earlier work from Argyris and Schon (1974, 1978). These can be flagged and named in sessions.

These are:

**Loop 1:** where the practitioner is acting and doing differently

**Loop 2:** where the practitioner is thinking and framing differently

**Loop 3:** where the practitioner is being different.

This also reads across to Kegan's Model of the Evolving Self (1985). Kegan argues that shifts in the levels of adult development are linked to shifts in our awareness and consciousness. These levels of adult development are described as:

**Level 1:** impulsive self

**Level 2:** self-centered

**Level 3:** self-reading

**Level 4:** self-authorizing

**Level 5:** self-transforming.

A common theme across all of these models is the message that the depth or levels of learning appear to be related to the nature and degree of change that becomes possible. This is shown below, where levels of reflection are mapped against possible stages in the development of the coach and coaching supervisor.

| Level of reflection | Type of reflective learning | Level of learning | Level of change | Stage of development |
|---|---|---|---|---|
| Participant | *Know what* | **Act differently** | *Surface* | **Foundation** |
| Reflection | *Know how* | **Think differently** | *Transactional* | **Practitioner** |
| Critical reflection | *Know why* | **Be different** | *Transformational* | **Mastery** |

*Understanding adult learners needs for trust and safety*

Bowlby's work on Attachment Theory (1988) has an important place in helping to understand what coaching supervisors bring to the relationship. Bowlby argued that infants thrive in trusted environments that are made safe and secure. Without this, insecure, avoidant and defended behaviors are played out that interfere with natural growth and development. Neuroscience research is also providing evidence about how the brain is able to develop new neural connections through supportive learning environments (Brown, 2011).

*Understanding the blocks to learning and change*

Reflective learning is not easy and requires huge personal courage.

While making sense of experiences can be fun, joyful and liberating it can also be painful, fearful and frightening as beliefs, assumptions, thoughts, feelings and behaviors are questioned and challenged and found to be no longer serving.

Feelings of inadequacy, guilt and shame also need to be worked through in order to free blocks, obstacles and past scripts. Central here is remembering that learning and change is an emotional, social and psychological process that must be handled, honored and respected with care, courage, clarity and compassion. Holding a Transition (and Grievance) model like that of Kubler Ross (1969) (see Figure 4.3), which emerged from the Hospice Movement, can help both the supervisee and the coaching supervisor to navigate the emotional process.

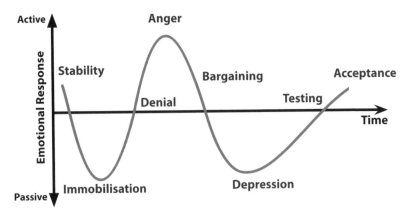

**Figure 4.3 -** *Transition Curve (adapted from Kubler Ross)*

*New Framework: "Tree of reflective learning"*

The author has attempted to pull together all of the different aspects of Reflective Learning in to a new framework which is called the "Tree of Reflective Learning".

The tree serves as a metaphor to try to capture and work through all of the different and complementary elements of reflective learning practice. This is where the tree's

▼ *branches represent "the What" of the Experience*
   *(for example: the action, event, feeling or unease)*

▼ *trunk represents "the How" of the Learning processes (capturing the different models, theories and approaches to learning)*

   and

▼ *roots represents "the Why" or making meaning from the learning experience and the choices made about the extent or embodiment of the learning and the change which can then occur (or not).*

**The branches**

**The trunk**

**The roots**

GROWING TREE OF CRAFTSMANSHIP © JUNKO MORI

**Illustration:** *"Tree of Reflective Learning"*

| The branches | The trunk | The roots |
|---|---|---|
| The *what* of the actual experience. | The *how* of the learning process. | The *why* of learning. |
| Triggers are:<br>• *an experience*<br>• *a noticing*<br>• *impressions*<br>• *disconnects*<br>• *an unease*<br>• *tensions*<br>to form stories. | Includes:<br>• *learning styles*<br>• *Kolb's Learning Cycle*<br>• *reflection **on** and **in** action*<br>• *actual v espoused theory*<br>• *stages, states and cycles of development*<br>• *secure base*<br>• *Blooms' taxonomy*<br>• *multiple intelligences*<br>• *Scharmer's Theory U*<br>• *transitions*<br>• *IQ, EQ and SQ*<br>• *systems thinking*<br>• *neuroscience.* | • *values*<br>• *worldview*<br>• *script*<br>• *wisdom*<br>• *authenticity*<br>• *integration*<br>• *congruence*<br>• *identity*<br>• *being.* |

## In their own words

Final thoughts on the power of reflective learning are offered by two coach supervisors.

As Amanda Edwards, executive coach and supervisor from the WorkLife Balance Center, says:

"So… what does reflective practice mean to me? Essentially, the opportunity to stand back from my work and see what has emerged. I have learned that the reflective process allows me to peel back the layers of an experience and observe the impact I had; it allows me to consider the interplay between my thoughts, my feelings and behavior and see how this connected with a client or group. I notice how often it offers the opportunity to humbly acknowledge that the outcome is often greater than the sum of the parts – the role of the spirit and intent that sits behind my work, the power of engaging with another human being and the learning that emerges from two (or more) of us working with common purpose. It also provides a challenging mirror to notice when my 'stuff' (ego etc) might start to get the in the way of a clear and authentic connection with the client.

Reflective practice has become the heartbeat of learning for me. It engages and stimulates me to reach beyond the surface of my coaching practice and to really consider how I might add value; specifically how the theoretical principles, quality of relationship, skills and intent all connect to create a powerful learning space for clients. Perhaps most importantly, reflective practice is wonderfully optimistic: always offering a new chance to reach out to the client from a place of growing awareness and presence to provide an atmosphere in which we might both grow."

As Maren Donata Urschel, coach and supervisor from Fruitful Coaching and co-founder of Leading from the Future©, says:

"Reflective practice has become an invaluable companion to me as a person and as a professional as I strongly believe that my ability to reflect has a direct impact on who I can become. Making sense of experiences in retrospect by allowing myself to think and feel what I may not have been able to fully express at the time enables me to take away what is useful to me and to leave what is not mine. And the wonderful thing about reflective practice is that there is always learning and the possibility of choice for the future – to do exactly the same again or to do it differently next time. To me this creates a deep sense of trust that every situation in my life is and has been worthwhile because – through reflective practice – it enables me to discover more about who I am. In this context the words 'failure' and 'success' become unimportant because the focus is on learning rather than on labeling.

"Reflective practice is also present in every interaction I have with my clients. I see part of my role as facilitating the quest for clarity on a situation that might have felt puzzling or just 'does not seem to go away' long after it has happened. Clarity through reflective practice increases self-awareness, generates choice for the future and enables clients to free up space and energy for new things to emerge. Often, providing a non-judgmental space for the client to think and feel what they were unable to bring to the surface in a given situation is already enough to enable them to move on."

Reflective learning practices are active, intentional and conscious processes that help us to develop practical wisdom and ways of knowing in the here and now toward desirable practice.

Through reflective learning practices it is possible for the practitioner to shift existing paradigms of self, beliefs, assumptions, knowledge and theory toward new insights and a deeper wisdom. By becoming reflective practitioners we insure that we engage wholeheartedly in our own learning unfolding stories of personal and professional development toward becoming more and more of who we truly are. Reflective learning thus becomes a way of being in the world that can infuse all aspects of our life and work.

Given the privileged nature of our work, learning to become reflective practitioners is both a professional and ethical obligation for coaches and coaching supervisors. This combines moral duty with fun, surprise and spontaneity to generate massive opportunities for personal and professional growth.

In this chapter you will have discovered that reflective learning practices are fundamental to all coaching and coaching supervision practice. Reflective learning is the lifeblood that drives creativity, inspiration and practical wisdom in practice, moment by moment.

Processes and theories have been shared. However, the emphasis has been on the qualities of the coaching supervisor to create a safe and creative space for reflective learning.

Given the privileged nature of our work, learning to become reflective practitioners is both a professional and ethical obligation for coaches and coaching supervisors.

## References

**Amulya, Joy (2003)** "What is reflective practice?", Center for Reflective Community Practice (CRCP), Massachusetts Institute of Technology (MIT), **www.supervisionandcoaching.com/pdf/ What%20is%20Reflective%20Practice%20(Amulya%202004).pdf,** accessed June 20, 2012.

**Belenky, M.F., Clinchy, B.M., Goldberger, N.R. and Tarule, J.M.. (1986),** *Women's Ways of Knowing.* Basic Books, NY.

**Bowlby, J (1988)** *A Secure Base: Parent–child attachment and healthy human development*, London, UK: Routledge.

**Boyd, E and Fales, A (1983)** "Reflective learning: Key to learning from experience", *Journal of Humanistic Psychology, 23(2):* pp. 99-117.

**Brown, P (2011)** "Interview with Professor Paul Brown", *The Bulletin of the Association for Coaching*, 6: pp. 3-7.

**English Oxford Dictionary (1976)** sixth edition, Oxford, UK : Oxford University Press.

**Gibbs, C (1988)** *Learning by Doing: A guide to teaching and learning methods*, Further

**Johns, C (2004)** *Becoming a Reflective Practitioner*, Oxford, UK: Blackwell Publishing.

**Kegan, R (1982)** *The Evolving Self: Problem and process in human development*, Massachusetts, US: Harvard University Press.

**Kolb, D (1984)** *Experiential learning: experience as the source of learning and development,* Englewood Cliffs, New Jersey, US: Prentice Hall.

**Kubler Ross, E (1969)** *On Death and Dying*, London, UK: Tavistock Publications Ltd.

**Luft, J.; Ingham, H. (1950).** "The Johari window, a graphic model of interpersonal awareness". *Proceedings of the western training laboratory in group development* (Los Angeles: UCLA).

**Mezirow, J (1990)** "How critical reflection triggers transformational learning", in J Mezirow *et al.* (eds), *Fostering Critical Reflection in Adulthood: A guide to transformative and emancipatory learning*, San Francisco, CA, US: Jossey-Boss, pp. 1-20.

**Rowley, J (2007)** "The wisdom hierarchy: Representations of the DIKW hierarchy", *Journal of Information Science, 33*, pp. 2-19.

**Scharmer, O (2007)** Theory U; Leading from the Future as it Emerges; The Social Technology of Presencing . Society of Organizational Learning pp 8.

**Schon. D (1983)** *The Reflective Practitioner: How professionals think in action*, US: Basic Books Ltd.

**Socrates (between 470 BC and 399 BC)** "Apologia 38a", http.// en.wikiquote.org, accessed September 15, 2011.

# 5 | *Mindfulness and presence in coaching supervision*

- Ian MacKenzie

OTHER CHAPTERS in this book speak of supervision as a reflective practice, involving working from the heart and incorporating a transpersonal context. This chapter shows how mindfulness and presence are essential qualities underpinning this work. It explores how applications of mindfulness range much further than the addressing of stress and tension, deeply informing the supervisory relationship and, through this, the practice of the supervisee and his or her service to the client. It explores and defines the quality of presence and shows how this relates to mindfulness, not only as a state of focused, non-judging perception, but also as a deep and wide heart-based awareness, allowing the supervisor and supervisee to access their deepest intuition. Finally, it explores practical ways for supervisors to develop a deeper sense of calm presence in themselves and the supervisee.

| 'Mindfulness' | a quality of gently focused awareness. |
|---|---|
| 'Presence' | the quality of total engagement and wide but precise awareness of the self and others. |

## The role of mindfulness and presence in the supervisory relationship

A recurrent theme of this book is the importance of the quality and the range of the supervisory relationship. This chapter looks at one of the key elements of that relationship – the quality of the supervisor's presence. The supervisee may be in search of many things: a teacher, a regulator, a mentor, a developer, an adviser, etc. An important facet of the early part of the supervisory relationship is to identify and clarify the supervisee's expectations and projections and to allow the relationship to develop within clear boundaries and realistic role expectations.

One of the supervisor's most important functions – explicit or implicit – is as role model. This is not an issue only of what the supervisor *does* in terms of his or her professionalism, clarity, reliability, access to resources, effective use of process and so on. It is, more importantly, how the supervisor *is*. "Who you are is how you supervise." Many of the aspects of supervision covered in this book require us as supervisors to:

▼ *Model openness, calmness and authenticity.*

▼ *Demonstrate a level of clarity about ourselves, the supervisee and the supervisee's client that will identify areas of parallel process and transference.*

▼ *Help the supervisee reflect on wider and deeper implications beyond a specific client or situation.*

▼ *Access deep levels of intuition and intuitive wisdom.*

▼ *Be prepared to operate in a field of 'not knowing' in which knowledge, understanding and wisdom can spontaneously arise.*

This is not a trivial undertaking. It requires the supervisor to continually develop the range and depth of his or her awareness. We will show here how the proper development of mindfulness can give rise to a broadening and deepening of this quality of presence.

## Mindfulness and presence in the Full Spectrum Model

In the Full Spectrum Model, mindfulness and presence are described among the meta-skills of supervision, relating to the segments of 'energy management', 'self-awareness and support', and 'coaching/counseling boundaries'. However, if we explore mindfulness and presence more deeply, it becomes clear that these are essential qualities underlying all other areas within the model. This is because they are the ground from which aspects like sensitivity to ethical issues, psychological mindedness and the development of effective supervisory relationships can arise.

| AREA OF MODEL | HOW MINDFULNESS AND PRESENCE CONTRIBUTE |
|---|---|
| Thinking/ Perspectives | Supports a breadth of vision and the ability to hold a whole-field awareness. |
| Meta-skills/ Self-support/ Reflection | Increases sensitivity and awareness of parallel process and other interpersonal issues. Supports presence and models the development of the internal supervisor. Enables space for reflection and develops a sense of self in supervision. |
| Relationship building and sustaining tasks | Enhances the development of trust, allows challenge within a safe space and supports the development of clarity around ethical and professional issues. |
| Tools and actions | Underlies the successful application of supervision tools and enhances appropriateness in the selection of tools. |

## Mindfulness and presence – definitions and relationship

First, we need to understand what our terms mean.

### Mindfulness – some background

The word 'mindfulness' is now in fairly common usage as a description of a certain state of mind or perception. Originally, the word came into use in this way from descriptions of Buddhist meditation. It is a translation of the Pali word 'sati' or Sanskrit 'smrti' and is usually related in the modern west to techniques of meditation – most commonly, the 'mindfulness of breathing'.

The current popularization of the term in a non-Buddhist context arose considerably from the work of John Kabat-Zinn and his work in the Stress Reduction Clinic and the Center for Mindfulness in Medicine, Health Care, and Society at the University of Massachusetts Medical School. Kabat-Zinn developed the meditation techniques he had learned as a Zen practitioner and combined them with elements of yoga to bring relief from pain and stress to patients. He called this Mindfulness Based Stress Reduction (MBSR).

In the UK, Kabat-Zinn's work was noticed and investigated by Clinical Psychologists searching for a way to help patients work with recurrent depression. This resulted in the development by J Mark, G Williams, John D Teasdale and Zindle V Segal of Mindfulness Based Cognitive Therapy (MBCT) (Kabat-Zinn, Segal, Williams and Teasdale 2006), a combination of Kabat-Zinn's approaches with processes and tools from cognitive therapy. This approach has been adopted by the NHS as a successful approach to preventing recurrent depression, and is currently being researched, taught and developed throughout the UK, notably at the University of Bangor.

Along with this secular medical development, Buddhist groups have continued to teach mindfulness meditation. While mindfulness is a foundational aspect of nearly all Buddhist practice, it has probably been most extensively promoted by the Vietnamese teacher Thich Nhat Hanh.

## What is mindfulness?

So what are all of these people – meditators, psychologists and therapists – talking about? What is this thing, this state, that we call 'mindfulness'?

This is actually a subject of some controversy and occasional contention. This is partly because we know it when we have it, but it is difficult to describe – like trying to tell someone who has never tasted salt what salt tastes like. But in the context of supervision and coaching, we can begin to explore some of its aspects. The examples we'll use are largely gleaned from supervisees in supervision – later we will explore the ramifications from the supervisor's position.

*Mindfulness is a state of being*

A common question asked by teachers during meditation sessions is, "Where is your mind now?" Mindfulness is about where your mind is *now*. It is about being fully and calmly aware of what is happening in the present, both outside and within oneself.

Many supervisees coming to supervision report a range of concerns that arise during coaching:

▼ *"Does this client like me? Will she come back?"*

▼ *"Am I giving value? How will I know?"*

▼ *"Am I out of my depth?"*

▼ *"I don't know what to ask/do next."*

▼ *"What process/technique do I need to introduce here? What if I haven't got one?"*

### Supervision scenario 1: **Jane**

Jane is a fairly new life coach. I've been working with her in supervision for about a month, looking at a range of issues around her relationship with her clients and building her confidence.

As the supervision sessions continue, I begin to notice themes arising in Jane's sessions. Above all there is insecurity about the value that she can bring to her clients, which leads her to anxiously look around for some new process or technique that will help them.

The ground of work shifts, and we begin to explore ways in which Jane can ground and center herself and simply be with her clients, offering them primarily the quality of her full presence and attention, the processes and techniques introduced sensitively and appropriately, and sometimes not at all.

The examples we have described are largely founded in anxiety – but this is not the only source of distracting mental activity in the coach. He or she can, for example:

▼ get 'hooked' into the client's mental games

▼ give so much attention to helping to solve the problem 'out there' that he or she fails to notice important information from the client's behaviors in the room

▼ get so caught up in the problem, situation, process or world that he or she becomes unaware of, or discounts, the client's emotional affect on him or her and the useful information that this may contain.

To mindfulness, this mental chatter is not in itself the issue. But the supervisee is working at less than his or her full capability if his or her emotional investment in the chatter is detracting from his or her ability to fully be with the client. He or she is also limiting his or her ability to access his or her own personal resources on the client's behalf, and in greater danger of falling prey to unhelpful collusions, game playing and projections.

Working mindfully, a coach will be aware of these tendencies as they arise, he or she will note them and he or she will choose whether or how to respond. But the focus of his or her attention will be the client and what is happening now – not only what the client is telling him or her, but how exactly the information is being conveyed, what impact it is having on him or her and how that may relate to what is happening in the rest of the client's world. His or her attitude, to quote John Welwood, is one of "warm wondering and gentle doggedness".

The amount of information arising within the session has not diminished – if anything it has increased. But it seems to arise in a state of unhurried spaciousness.

## Mindfulness has breadth and depth as well as focus

One common misconception about mindfulness is that it is simply focusing on one thing at a time. Certainly, this is an important aspect and it is commonly taught initially in this way: Thich Nhat Hanh describes eating a segment of orange with total awareness of the taste, texture and scent of the experience, with no thought of what came before or what will come after. In MBCT training, the orange segment has morphed into a raisin, but the principle is the same.

However, it should be clear from the description above that mindfulness is not just a one-pointed, deliberate, focused attention. It is about awareness – where attention is directed in the context of wide background awareness. It is a space of clear vision where the mind is not clinging or caught up, but can work with the issue at hand without distraction while monitoring a whole range of background information. Kosho Uchiyama, a Japanese Zen teacher, uses the analogy of driving a car: Attention is always on the road ahead, but there is a continual and responsive awareness of the scenery on each side.

This wide-ranging aspect of mindfulness will feature again when we look at its relationship to the quality of presence.

### Supervision scenario 2: **Tony**

Tony is a leadership coach in a public sector organization. He has been coming to supervision sessions for some years, and is generally confident and open to developing his coaching practice.

However, in this session he is clearly troubled. It emerges that he is feeling pressured and has somehow failed as a coach. His corporate HR sponsor and his client's line manager have complained that they can see no signs of the behavior changes in his client that they were expecting.

Tony is bemused – his client has consistently reported how he has changed his approach and is achieving good results.

Doing this supervision with a quality of calm and presence allows Tony to feel accepted, puts the situation into a wider context and allows the space to open into a wider view of the situation. We begin to explore the Seventh Eye from the Seven Eyed Model – the wider organizational context in which this is happening, and Tony begins to see more clearly that there are structural and political issues clouding the problem. He relaxes, and we begin to explore how he may deal with these to resolve the current situation and prevent it in future.

For the supervisee, this ability to observe and work with multiple levels of information in a calm and focused way develops his or her capability to effectively apply both emotional and cognitive intelligences. It enables the supervisee to ask specific and probing questions, refer to the wider context and deepen the client's awareness by reflecting behaviors, themes and patterns of which the client may be unaware

## Mindfulness is about engaging with our experience

One criticism of some mindfulness approaches is that they can encourage the practitioner to become a detached observer. Matthieu Ricard recently pointed out that even a sniper has to be highly mindful and "in the flow" in terms of his or her concentration and focus on his or her intention. A distorted application of mindfulness can lead to an apparently emotionless observer, sitting beyond and outside the messiness of human interaction. A coach using mindfulness in this way would be highly focused and aware but without real engagement.

In a recent coaching workshop, one of the students was participating in an exercise where he was asked to simply sit silently with full mindfulness and presence while his 'client' talked through the issue they were bringing to coaching. At the end of the exercise, the student was asked to feed back his reactions. He gave an in-depth account of his minute observations of his 'client's' body language, tone of voice, shifts of behavior, etc. It was very accurate, complete and professional.

But when he was asked how he was feeling in the session, and how he sensed that his 'client' may be feeling, he was nonplussed. His sense of mindful presence was that of a detached and highly attentive but somewhat clinical observer.

True mindfulness involves the heart. Its range includes the emotions – in fact, awareness of feelings is an essential and traditional aspect of mindfulness. Awareness of emotion is an essential component of emotional intelligence. The proper development of mindfulness gives better access to our emotional states.

## What is presence?

The examples used above are largely *intra-personal*. They relate to the experience of the coach as being more or less mindfully engaged with the client. It could be argued that presence is the *inter-personal* experience of being in contact with a mindful state of being in another. However, to really begin to understand presence, we have to delve a little deeper.

First we can explore some definitions:

*"Presence is a state of awareness, in the moment, characterised by the felt experience of timelessness, connectedness and a larger truth."* **(Silsbee, 2008: 21)**

*"Ability to be fully conscious and create spontaneous relationship with the client."*
**(International Coach Federation Competencies B4)**

*"[A] deep listening, of being beyond one's preconceptions and historical ways of making sense."*
**(Senge cited in Senge, Scharmer, Jaworski and Flowers, 2005)**

*"Presence is when you're no longer waiting for the next moment, believing that the next moment will be more fulfilling than this one."* **(Tolle, 2005)**

*"Presence is also intimacy. Two human beings present together experience intimacy and knowledge of one another, and each person understands something of the other's story and, consequently, their humanity."* **(Rodenburg, 2007: 4)**

*"Presence is an alive and freeing state of generous, compassionate and mindful awareness in our being – which is felt and experienced – in the here and now in the relationship with another; and which opens our hearts, minds and bodies to a wider reality and a joyful field of connectedness, possibility and potential."* **(Patterson, 2011: 120)**

There are many others, but this brief selection shows that, as with mindfulness, there is no commonly accepted, precise definition. On the other hand, the definitions also suggest that all of these writers are groping toward describing a similar experience or state. The differences often arise out of what they are prepared to claim for this state.

As with mindfulness, we can set out from these definitions to explore some of the key features of presence.

*Presence is being here now*

If we take a simple approach to definition, presence is about *being present*. Or, *not being absent*, wholly or in part. Just as when the school child calls out "present" in answer to a roll call. But being present is not just about being in the room. It is being fully present, with oneself, the surrounding environment, the other in the room, without distraction from mental chatter and noise.

This has a clear relationship to the mindful awareness described earlier – it is a related state. An important feature of presence, however, is that it is *relational* – the inner state of mindful awareness is subtly communicated to and experienced by others. Not only are we fully present with and fully aware of the other person in the room – he or she knows this. This implies a congruity between external expression – which very much includes silence – and a state of heart/mind.

*Presence is not necessarily about 'impact'*

People in sales and corporate leadership roles have often used the term 'presence' to signify a quality of immediate impact that demands attention from others. Used in this way, the term relates to elements like 'gravitas' and 'charisma'. This is the area of Patsy Rodenburg's "Third Circle". There is no doubt that true Presence – in this context, cognate with Rodenburg's "Second Circle" – can create impact – however, by our definition, impact is achieved not by the extension of ego or personality, but by the extension of awareness.

For example, I was a delegate at an Association for Neuro-Linguistic Programming conference a few years ago. Alexander Caillet took the floor for a session immediately after lunch. As he rose to speak, people were still re-entering with clattering coffee cups, reconnecting with their neighbors, finding their seats and their papers. Caillet stood and waited. He took in the whole room, sweeping everyone with a relaxed, friendly gaze. And he waited – although there was no sense in which we felt that he was waiting *for* anything. And gradually the attention of the whole room became focused on him. And yet he still said nothing, surveying the delegates calmly and unhurriedly. And then, as they all sat in hushed expectation, he began.

The point of this story is not that he got the audience's attention far more effectively than by imposing his personality from the rostrum by calling out, or tapping a glass, etc. – although this is true. The point is that he modeled a calm state of attentive awareness into which his audience were drawn in an attitude of warm curiosity. He seemed more interested in them than in himself.

Dogen, the thirteenth-century Japanese teacher and philosopher, said:

> *"To study the Way is to study yourself.*
> *To study yourself is to forget yourself."*
>
> **Dogen**

Similarly, in a state of true presence we are highly aware of our own process, but it does not dominate. We have to 'forget our self', or 'get out of our own way'.

### Presence leads into the unknown

If presence has a purpose, it is to create a field in which creativity and insight may manifest. It is not about 'fixing' anything – although solutions may arise.

For example, the supervisee rushes into supervision with a mind full of 'stories' about a particular crisis with a client organization. The supervisor can either:

▼ collude with this mental state, working with the supervisee on fixes, solutions and strategies, or

▼ by the simple calm but deeply concerned quality of his or her presence, invite the supervisee into a wider, more spacious view where the problem becomes more proportional. Solutions may arise out of this space but, even if they do not, the supervisee has been able to access a capability for openness and reflection from which action will probably materialize in the future.

### Supervision scenario 3: **Alan**

Alan is a very experienced leadership coach. His background is in sales, and he is highly results-oriented. He is often very successful in the environment in which he works, particularly in developing his client's skills in analysis and clarity of thinking.

However, occasionally Alan comes up against a situation where his usual approaches do not work, and he becomes confused and flustered.

In supervision, it becomes clear that Alan is not effectively acc-essing his own emotional intelligence. He tends to re-gard his own feelings as irrelevant, preferring to rely on his analytical intelligence.

We work together to develop his mindfulness of feelings – both his own and his clients. We then begin to explore how he can use this new source of information effectively in coaching. From there, over a number of sessions, we develop his ability to be present in the room, less results-oriented and leaving an open space where his clients can express and explore their own emotions.

### Presence, presencing and Theory U

This principle is the foundation of Scharmer's "Theory U" **(Senge, Scharmer, Jaworski and Flowers, 2005).** (See Figure 4.3.)

Scharmer's approach, recently elaborated from *Presence* into his more recent book, *Theory U*, introduces a process that he calls "presencing". Put simply, the first part of the U process involves a progressive letting go of fixed thought, fixed feelings and fixed goals and sense of self. Underlying this is the principle that in any situation the future is emerging into awareness. Presencing allows that future to manifest – but not if we hang on to fixed truths, alliances or a sense of who we are. (Scharmer has called the process of clinging to a fixed sense of self, "Absencing".)

The second part of the U transforms the emergent thinking into action.

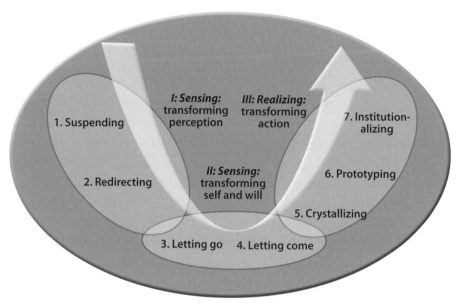

**Figure 4.3 -** *Scharmer's "Theory U"*

Scharmer's work with his associates has been largely around leadership and the development of socially responsive organizations. But it is easy to see how Theory U can be applied to the coaching and supervisory context. This demands a much fuller treatment than can be given here; we will just emphasize this progressive process of – not acquiring and constructing – but letting go and allowing to manifest. For the supervisor and supervisee, this may mean:

▼ *taking a more open view of situations*
  *– identifying and setting aside perceptual filters*

▼ *being prepared to engage deeply and empathetically*

▼ *renouncing goal-orientation and trusting in*
  *emergence and manifestation*

▼ *being prepared to 'forget the self' so that a deeper*
  *and more profound knowing can emerge.*

This requires the supervisor to support the supervisee through periods of uncomfortable ambiguity and uncertainty – to learn to be in a space of not-knowing. In environments and with supervisees who are highly outcome driven this can be particularly sensitive work and requires a good sense of appropriateness and timing. However, to ignore this field of emergent wisdom is to deny the supervisee access to a great source of transformative potential and to collude with his or her potential 'absencing'. This is a theme that we will return to when we look at developing mindfulness and presence in the supervisor and supervisee.

## The relationship between mindfulness and presence

From the descriptions so far, it is clear that mindfulness and presence share a common ground. However, they are also clearly not the same thing. Descriptions of the state of presence extend wider and deeper than those associated with mindful awareness. It seems to be possible to be mindfully aware without being present, but not possible to be present without being mindfully aware.

### Presence as the development of insight

One way of developing a better understanding of the relationship between the two may be to 'go back to the source'. In Buddhist teaching from all major streams, a differentiation is made between two forms of meditation:

| | | |
|---|---|---|
| **Shamatha**<br>*(Sanskrit)* | 'Calm abiding' or 'Stopping' | **Shamatha** meditation reduces mental chatter, reduces negative mental states like anxiety and anger, and develops clear, lucid clarity of thought. |
| **Vipashyana**<br>*(Sanskrit)* | 'Insight' or 'Seeing' | **Vipashyana** meditation leads to insight into the nature of reality. |

Generally it is believed that calming or stopping the discursive, distracted mind is a necessary precursor to developing insight.

It may be possible to extend this classification to mindfulness and presence. Clearly, mindfulness as taught in modern applications like MBCT is a calming process. We suggest that the development of presence is a *Vipashyana* practice – a practice of learning to 'See'. Presence, then, is a form of insight. Mindful awareness is the ground from which presence can emerge.

In practical terms, this allows us to create an integrated model of mindfulness and presence that the supervisor can use to monitor his or her own internal state and that of the supervisee.

## An integrated model of mindfulness and presence

We have developed the following model (see Figure 4.4) both to show the relationship between mindfulness and presence and to provide a practical way of monitoring internal states.

It uses commonly found terms, such as 'focus' and 'awareness', in specific ways to provide an accessible terminology.

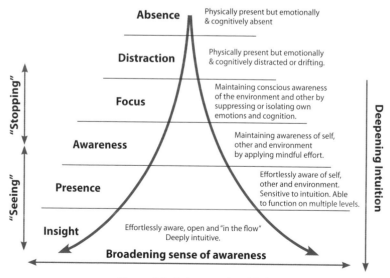

**Figure 4.4:** *An integrated model of mindfulness and presence*
© Ian Mackenzie 2011

This is a diagram that flows down and wide rather than up and narrow. This mimics the felt experience of deeper and broader awareness. The boundaries between these states are shown for convenience – in reality, states shade into one another and individuals move up and down between adjacent states.

The following descriptions use examples from the indicative behavior and experience of a supervision. It should be clear that the same indicators can be applied by the supervisor to the supervisee to monitor and work with his or her state.

## Absence

▼ *Physically present but emotionally and cognitively absent*

This is a commonly experienced state, especially by those under stress or emotionally distressed. Thoughts are wandering; feelings are overwhelming. The individual is living a scenario almost entirely within his or her own mind: 'daydreaming', remembering or fantasizing. This is the more extreme end of Rodenburg's "First Circle".

The supervisor will present as looking into the distance, as struggling to make eye contact and he or she may have to be frequently recalled to the present in order to interact at all.

## Distraction

▼ *Physically present but emotionally and cognitively distracted or drifting*

To a greater or lesser extent, this is probably the most common state of mind for most people. There is a degree of presence, but there is constant interference from extraneous thoughts and feelings. These are not thoughts or feelings deliberately engaged – thoughts arise unbidden and emotions intrude on the present from the past or from imagined future scenarios.

The supervisor may have difficulty keeping on track, may have short periods of 'absence' or he or she may simply not seem to be fully engaged.

## Focus

▼ *Maintaining conscious awareness of the environment and other by suppressing or isolating own emotions and cognition*

This is the first state that can be properly called mindful. The individual is maintaining a practiced effort in recognizing and suppressing distracting thoughts and feelings in order to maintain focus.

The supervisor may well be professional, attentive and apparently engaged, but the supervisee may sense a certain lack of authenticity – energy is being used to suppress distraction by elements not in the room. There is a feeling of effort and the unspecified unspoken. This can sometimes be evidenced in the 'corporate' or 'professional mask'.

## *Awareness*

▼ *Maintaining awareness of self, other and environment by applying mindful effort*

This encompasses what may be described as true mindfulness. Effort is involved, but thoughts and emotions are not suppressed – they are acknowledged as they arise and allowed to either inform or to drop away of their own accord while attention is gently maintained on the present.

The supervisor will be engaged, appropriately reflective, open and authentic. There will be a feeling of spaciousness and unhurried exploration. Deeper themes and issues may manifest in this open space.

### Presence

▼ *Effortlessly aware of self, other and environment*

▼ *Sensitive to intuition*

▼ *Able to function on multiple levels*

This state is natural and flowing. There is no sense of technique or effort. Thoughts and feelings arise in a relaxed spaciousness, like clouds in a clear blue sky. Intuitive insights, connections and themes emerge. There is a feeling of being grounded, secure and at ease. Distracting emotions and thoughts either disappear or are experienced as unobtrusive, low level background noise. There is an increasing sense of unity between the self, other and environment.

The supervisor will be engaged, resourceful and open to exploration. He or she will be able to access, trust and effectively interpret his or her own intuitive wisdom. He or she will be comfortable with periods of reflective silence and not knowing.

### Insight

▼ *Effortlessly aware, open and 'in the flow'*

▼ *Deeply intuitive*

In this state, clarity, openness and deep empathy are natural states in which we rest. Action arises spontaneously from the energy that manifests – there is little or no sense of making a decision or calculation.

If this energy is powerfully present in the room, supervision then becomes a dance where both parties are moving and responding to the same unheard music. Neither may know where this dance is taking them, but there is complete trust in the process and the emergent energy.

Another way of describing this emergent wisdom, to echo Otto Scharmer, is the transferring of the center of gravity from the self, with its anxieties, preferences and defenses, to the Self, with its wide sense of interconnection and interdependence.

## Developing mindfulness and presence in the supervisor and the supervisee

There are many available sources exploring the development of mindfulness and presence – including Buddhist or secularly adapted meditation as taught by Thich Nhat Hanh, John Kabat-Zinn, Pema Chodron and others; and practices for the development of presence and insight as advocated by Patsy Rodenburg, Catherine Ingram, Doug Silsbee and many more.

If the emergence of the quality of presence rests on the development of mindfulness, it is possible to suggest a structured approach beginning with mindfulness practice to calm and focus the mind, and then developing deeper and more sensitive awareness and confidence, allowing the arising and development of presence.

This does not mean that supervisors, coaches and others who demonstrate presence have necessarily engaged in mindfulness training. As many teachers like Sogyal Rinpoche and Shenpen Hookham suggest, echoed by Patsy Rodenburg, the mindful state is natural. It has become obscured in most of us – but less so in some than others. It is therefore possible for many people to engage this natural state under certain conditions – maybe when coaching, for example, but not when the car breaks down.

However – most of us can speak, but there is no-one who cannot be trained to speak more effectively. In developing mindfulness we are not creating something new. We are uncovering and rediscovering a natural resource and learning in order to employ it more effectively.

## Approaches to developing mindfulness

### Mindfulness meditation

The fundamental and most common practice for developing mindfulness is what is called 'meditation'. However, the word 'meditation' is a western coinage that can cover a wide range of practices. One supervisee commented that she meditated regularly. When her supervisor inquired more closely, it emerged that her meditation consisted of imagining herself in a beautiful, friendly, warm and loving environment.

While this has much value, it is not what is meant here. The heart of mindfulness meditation is to bring us closer to our immediate felt experience in a way that allows us to experience it and be effective within it.

Meditation, as we discuss it here, could be described as an establishing practice. The point is not to achieve a calm and relaxed state during the meditation – although this may happen and has benefits of its own. The point is, by regular meditation, to achieve a *habit* of mindfulness. In Tibetan, the word most commonly used for meditation is '*gom*'. 'Gom' can be roughly translated as '*get used to*'. The point is to make a relaxed, alert mindfulness a natural state for the mind to return to – a kind of default position.

## Try this

*Breath meditation*

▼ *Sit comfortably – preferably in an upright and alert but relaxed position. There is no need to sit cross-legged or on the floor – but you can if you like…*

▼ *You may prefer to close your eyes. Briefly scan your body – just notice areas of tension. Maybe take a couple of deep breaths, making a long exhalation through the mouth.*

▼ *When you are comfortable, bring your attention to your breath. Don't try to change it and don't run a commentary on it. Just rest your attention on your breath. If your mind wanders – and it will – as soon as you notice, bring your attention back to your breathing. It doesn't matter how often your mind wanders off – mindfulness is all about gentle, patient persistence. The mindfulness is in the noticing and coming back.*

▼ *If you find you're getting bored, irritated or anxious – this is just more stuff. Notice it, let it go and return to the breath.*

The simplest – and probably most commonly taught – form of mindfulness meditation is mindfulness of breathing. The example gives a simple set of instructions – fuller descriptions can be found in the books cited in the References.

Regular sessions of this practice, even for as little as 10 to 15 minutes a day, will have results, although by far the best way of developing the practice is to work with an experienced teacher who can give you help in working with difficulties – and there probably will be difficulties. Our minds are trained to a habit of distraction – "distracted by distraction from distraction" as TS Eliot put it. Mindfulness meditation is not just about learning the habit of mindfulness – it is also about unlearning the habit of distraction.

## Developing mindfulness in everyday life

Many mindfulness teachers – and particularly Thich Nhat Hanh – stress the importance of creating habits of mindfulness in day-to-day life. When walking, waiting at traffic lights or in queues, etc., we can develop the habit of taking in what is happening around us in a mindful way, rather than:

▼ *thinking about the future – when the lights will change, how long it will be before we are at the head of the queue, how we wish we were better prepared for our forthcoming supervision session…*

▼ *running a commentary on the present – how awful it is on the Tube, how totally unacceptable it is for our train to be delayed again, how our feet, legs, back, head hurt, how we hate crowds…*

▼ *reimagining the past – how we wish we'd said X, how we maybe should have traveled via Y, how funny our sister-in-law was in the pub on Friday…*

Of course, these thoughts, or our versions of them, will intrude. But, as in meditation, we note them without getting caught up in them and return our attention to what is going on around us and within us with a gentle, mindful curiosity. Life is constantly arising, manifesting and recreating itself all around us all the time – it is a shame to miss the show.

*Mindful moments*

There are a number of brief exercises we can do to intentionally 'bring the mind home' – particularly when we feel scattered or need to focus resources – before a difficult supervision, for example.

The following two examples are drawn from The Coaching Supervision Academy and MBCT (Kabat-Zinn, Segal, Williams and Teasdale, 2006), respectively. The habit of mindfulness cannot be acquired overnight – but gentle persistence can achieve much.

## Try this

*Grounding, Centering, Breathing*

### Grounding

Whether you are walking or sitting, become aware of where the 'ground' touches your body – through the soles of your feet, the back of your legs and bum, and your back. Bring all of your attention to that physical sensation for a moment. Feel the ground holding you up.

### Centering

Now bring all of your attention and awareness closer to home – to the trunk of your body. Be in the center of your body – let the trunk straighten and feel its strength.

### Breathing

Finally, bring your awareness to your breath. – let your breath breathe you. Notice the rise and fall of your chest or the flow of air as it enters and exits your nose. Ride on the breath.

*Practice this sequence slowly and regularly until you are able to use it effectively in a few seconds. Use it in your life and before and during supervision sessions.*

**Edna Murdoch, Coaching Supervision Academy, © 2004**

## Try this

*The three-minute breathing space*

This can be practiced as a regular thing two or three times a day – just to get into the habit.

### *Awareness*

Bring yourself into the present moment by deliberately adopting an erect and dignified posture. If possible, close your eyes. Then ask, "What is my experience right now... in thoughts... in feelings... in bodily sensations?"

Acknowledge and register your experience, even if it's unwanted.

### *Gathering*

Then, gently redirect full attention to breathing, to each in-breath and to each out-breath as they follow, one after the other.

Your breath can function as an anchor to bring you into the present and can help you tune into a state of awareness and stillness.

### *Expanding*

Expand the field of our awareness around your breathing, so that it includes a sense of the body as a whole, your posture and facial expression.

## Approaches to developing presence

Strictly speaking, it could be argued that presence cannot be developed – it is a state that naturally arises on the basis of habitual mindfulness. However, there are activities that can help bring the mind home. Many can be found in the work of the authors cited previously. Elaine Patterson, in *Supervision in Coaching: Supervision, ethics and continuous professional development* (2011), has a number of exercises and self-assessments for developing and monitoring the state of presence.

Here we offer a general, day-to-day approach and specific activities in preparing, during and after supervision.

## Try this

*Day-to-day presence*

The habit of mindfulness can in itself lead to the arising of presence:

▼ *observing the world and our own thoughts and emotions with an open curiosity*

▼ *taking time, in nature or even in a busy city, simply to sit and observe what arises – what feelings and thoughts are triggered by certain faces, sights or events*

▼ *in meetings, sitting back where appropriate, simply observing interactions without analysis or judgment*

▼ *when making decisions, suspending critique and analysis and bringing our attention to what our heart says*

▼ *looking up at the sky and out at the horizon more than we look at the ground and our feet*

▼ *closing our eyes and listening to the world without analyzing or thinking about the sounds we hear – simply letting them be. Then shifting our attention from the sounds to the silence from which they emerge and to which they return.*

## Before a supervision session

The 'Three-minute breathing space' exercise or the 'Grounding, Centering and Breathing' exercise are excellent ways to center ourselves before a session.

After that we can develop a sense of presence with the following exercise (developed from Hookham's meditation instructions (or 'hints' as she prefers to call them)).

*We may think of ourselves as clearing or preparing the space, inside us and outside us, in which the session will take place.*

## Try this

| PRESENCE HINTS | |
|---|---|
| **Being awake** | *Developing a sense of alert, undistracted, awareness (the preliminary exercise should have helped with this).* |
| **Touching your heart** | *Directing awareness to how we are feeling – in general, about ourselves and about the supervisee we are about to see. Not thinking about, analyzing or critiquing this – just briefly noticing it.* |
| **Being present** | *Being in the room with a general sense of spacious awareness.* |
| **Letting go** | *As thoughts and feelings arise, we note and observe them, and then, as we breathe out, we let them go into the surrounding space and out beyond the horizon.* |

(Hookham, 2006)

## During supervision

▼ *Working within that space we have created, note when we feel rushed, pressured, confused, irritated, etc. We note what we feel – it is valuable information – without being caught up in it.*

▼ *Being prepared to work with silence, to create a safe space in which the supervisee can reflect. Working in a way that allows insight to emerge, rather than trying to create it.*

▼ *Being sensitive to signals coming from inside us and outside us. Return sometimes to the heart – what is our heart telling us at this point?*

▼ *Being prepared to sit with not-knowing in the confidence that awareness and understanding are in the room and that they will manifest in their own time if we get out of the way.*

## After supervision

As part of our reflection on the session, we note how we are feeling. Then we return to the place of knowing within us and observe what we find there.

Then, on a long out-breath, we let this session go.

## Developing mindfulness and presence in the supervisee

Clearly, any of the techniques and activities above can be applied to coaching as much as to supervision. The supervisor can mentor the supervisee as appropriate to learn these approaches. We can also begin and end sessions with some breathing or other mindfulness activity, like the 'Three-minute breathing space'.

### Modeling mindfulness and presence

However, the most important developmental method, and the foundation for all of the others, is *modeling*. Through this, the supervisee can experience the *inter-personal* effects of a mindful approach: the experience of being in the presence of full, kind, mindful attention. This is because – to reiterate – mindfulness is not a process or technique – it is a state of being. It is best learned through experience. Through experiencing the mindful awareness of the supervisor, the supervisee begins to access his or her own resources of mindfulness and also begins to understand how this clear, calm presence can affect a client.

### Developing the courage not to know

An important aspect of supervision is to develop the supervisee's awareness of and confidence in his or her own resources as a human being, beyond knowledge, skill or technique. This is not to say that knowledge, skill and technique are not important but that they need to be employed in service of an attuned and sensitive awareness.

There is a strong tendency for coaches to reach into their 'bag of tricks' as if it contained a lifeline. One experienced supervisee, when approached even informally about an issue or problem, would immediately respond, "Oh, you need the six-step reframing tool for X" or "Have you got well-defined outcomes for what you want here?", etc. The response from the other person, spoken or silent, was often, "Well no – I really just wanted to talk about it."

Another, less experienced life coach, would spend hours fretting about not having a process or technique to offer a client, so that by the time the client arrived she was tense and anything but present.

Techniques, processes and models are very valuable in coaching, but one of the most valuable contributions a supervisor can make is to develop the supervisee's confidence in his or herself and his or her own inner resources. This helps him or her to simply be present with his or her client and to reach for the appropriate resource when he or she needs it.

## Conclusion

It is possible to be an effective supervisor at some levels without developing the qualities we have discussed here. However, we would suggest that the development of mindfulness and presence is essential in order to work with the range and depth implied by the Full Spectrum Model.

An essential part of our job as supervisors is to develop the resourcefulness of coaches. The development of mindfulness and presence widens the coach's access to his or her own personal resources and the quality of his or her own unique presence with his or her clients.

The coach, modeling this for clients, can have a transformative effect. From those clients, that effect passes on to the wider world. So, the effective modeling of mindfulness and presence in supervision can have far-reaching effects.

### *What you have discovered in this chapter*

▼ *what mindfulness and presence are and how they are related their importance in coaching supervision*

▼ *ways to develop and employ mindfulness in day-to-day life and in the supervision setting*

▼ *how mindfulness is the foundation of presence and the levels of mindfulness and presence that can be manifested in relationship to others*

▼ *ways to develop and enhance the quality of presence in the supervisor and coach.*

## REFERENCES

**Dogen, Ehei trans Tanahashi, Kazuaki (1986)** *Moon in a Dewdrop: Writings of Zen Master Dogen* North Point Press, New York

**Hookham, Shenpen (2006)** *Introduction to Formless Meditation.* The Shrimala Trust, Criccieth

**Ingram, Catherine (2003)** *Passionate Presence* Element, Portland Oregon

**Kabat-Zinn, Jon; Segal, Zindel V., Williams, J. Mark G.; Teasdale, John D.** **(2006)** *Mindfulness-based Cognitive Therapy for Depression: A New Approach to Preventing Relapse.* Guildford Press, New York & London

**Kabat-Zinn, Jon (2004)** *Wherever You Go, There You are: Mindfulness Meditation for Everyday Life* Piatkus, London

**Patterson, Elaine (2011)** in *Supervision in Coaching: Supervision, Ethics and Continuous Professional Development* ed. Jonathan Passmore; Kogan Page and Association for Coaching, London

**Rodenburg, Patsy (2007),** *Presence*, Penguin, London

**Senge Peter: Sharmer, C Otto; Jaworski, Joseph; Flowers, Betty Sue (2005),** *Presence* Nicholas Brearley, London & Boston

**Silsbee, Douglas (2008)** *Presence-Based Coaching*, Jossey-Bass, San Francisco

**Sogyal Rinpoche (1994)** *Meditation: A Little Book of Wisdom.* Harper Collins, San Francisco

**Thich Nhat Hanh (1999),** *Peace Is Every Step: The Path of Mindfulness in Everyday Life.* Rider, London

**Tolle, Eckhart (2005)** *A New Earth*, Penguin, London

# 6 | *Coaching supervision - a psychodynamic approach*

- Kate Lanz

PSYCHODYNAMICS IS the study of mental processes from a dynamic point of view. The approach assumes that the psyche is deep, complex and in constant motion. The dynamic aspect of the approach refers to the subtle interplay between the conscious and unconscious minds as certain emotions get pushed from the conscious into the unconscious mind, seemingly without our knowledge.

In my supervision and in my coaching work, a psychodynamic approach is one of a number of approaches that I use and I find it very effective. One of the particular benefits of a psychodynamic approach is that it enables both the coach and the supervisor to work deeply, quickly. It is an approach that can be skillfully used by non-clinicians with proper preparation, thought and supervision.

In supervision, a psychodynamic approach helps to derive insight from the dynamic connection between the psychological and emotional aspects of the relationships in question. These are the relationship between the coach and his or her client, the relationship between the coach and the supervisor, as well as that between the client and his or her organization.

## A psychodynamic perspective and the Full Spectrum Model

The aim of the Full Spectrum Model (see Figure 6.1) is to support supervisors to use a wide and rich multilayered framework in their supervision work. It encompasses a broad number of fields of awareness and knowledge and it attends to the coach, the client and the system of which they are all part. The approaches at the heart of the FSM are dynamic, they consider relationships within a system and they are highly reflective; a psychodynamic approach plays very strongly in many of the elements of the FSM. The elements of the FSM are outlined below.

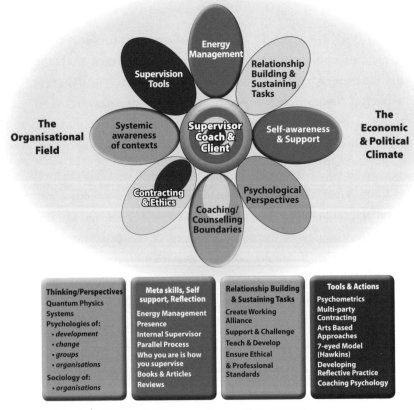

The Organisational Field

Energy Management

Supervision Tools

Relationship Building & Sustaining Tasks

Systemic awareness of contexts

Supervisor Coach & Client

Self-awareness & Support

The Economic & Political Climate

Contracting & Ethics

Coaching/ Counselling Boundaries

Psychological Perspectives

| Thinking/Perspectives | Meta skills, Self support, Reflection | Relationship Building & Sustaining Tasks | Tools & Actions |
|---|---|---|---|
| Quantum Physics | Energy Management | Create Working Alliance | Psychometrics |
| Systems | Presence | Support & Challenge | Multi-party Contracting |
| Psychologies of: | Internal Supervisor | Teach & Develop | Arts Based Approaches |
| · development | Parallel Process | Ensure Ethical & Professional Standards | 7-eyed Model (Hawkins) |
| · change | Who you are is how you supervise | | Developing Reflective Practice |
| · groups | Books & Articles | | Coaching Psychology |
| · organisations | Reviews | | |
| Sociology of: | | | |
| · organisations | | | |

© COACHING SUPERVISION ACADEMY **www.coachingsupervisionacademy.com**

**Figure 6.1** - *Full Spectrum Model*

This chapter looks in some detail at two different case studies brought by two different coaches to supervision. My aim is to bring to life the supervision session from the inside, highlighting my use of the psychodynamic in support of the coach's learning and in the service of the client. The reader will see many of the key aspects of the FSM evidenced by this psychodynamic approach in these supervision cases.

In order to be very clear, I focus my explanation here mainly on the psychodynamic concepts being used and their practical application in the supervision session, but indicate also how these fit within the FSM. I hope I can encourage supervisors unfamiliar with the approach to explore it more fully with a view to developing their interest in its use in supervision.

## Tension between personal motivation and the work task

This case introduces JD, an experienced coach who, having left industry, developed himself as a coach and has run his own successful practice for the last five years.

This case study explores:

▼ the defense mechanism of denial to defend against anger

▼ parallel process: using the unconscious links between the supervisor–supervisee relationship and the supervisee–client relationship to gain insight into the client's inner world

▼ anxiety in the coachee and the coach and how this can be used to help the coach understand the client's inner world

▼ countertransference: the coach's emotional response
to the client

▼ techniques that the coach can use in the next session
to gently and unthreateningly surface the anger in
order to mobilize the coachee's power in relation to
the task without the coachee becoming upset
or defensive.

JD wanted to discuss his new client, Diana, in the session.
He had just had their first meeting. He was excited at
being invited to coach at this new firm and he was keen
to establish himself there.

Diana was a junior partner at a large accountancy
firm. She had a particular technical focus. She was a
very warm, engaging person who had recently had a
performance review where she had been told that while
her technical delivery was solid her overall performance
was considered to "only just meets expectations" and that
she really must increase her business development for
the firm. She was otherwise at risk of being considered
one of the weaker partners and there would ultimately
be consequences to that.

Diana spent much of her time designing and delivering
development programs for younger associates in her
area of the business, which was one of the largest in the
firm. She had a tremendous capacity to teach. This was
where her real passion and energy clearly lay. When JD
relayed how Diana had described this development work
his voice became more energetic and he sat forward in
his chair. I had a real image of Diana before me.

JD had then worked effectively and quickly to get Diana to articulate what she felt the business development and financial goals that the firm were expecting may be. The targets were stretching and were a very long way off what she was currently delivering. JD had also established the likely time frame that the firm had in mind for Diana to deliver these financial results. I caught myself feeling that this was a really tall order. Diana herself had verbally expressed only mild frustration at the targets, very much in passing, saying that she hoped they would not take her attention too much away from spending time on the associate work. The fact that I had had quite a strong and worried reaction to the size of the task facing her and that JD had reported at this point only "mild frustration" at the targets, put me on alert listening for denial as a defense response in the coaching client.

*Key concept –* **denial as a defense mechanism**

**KEY CONCEPT**

In the psychodynamic model, denial is a central defense mechanism. When denial is happening the person pushes away the uncomfortable feelings, which he or she does not want to look at, into the unconscious part of his or her mind. These difficult feelings are, however, still quite close to the surface. They are not totally repressed and hidden. The coach will therefore catch a glimpse of them if he or she listens out and reads body language carefully.

It was clear from JD's body language and the energy with which he reported some aspects of the session and the lack of energy in reporting others that JD was tuning in much more readily to the positive feelings that the client was demonstrating. JD appeared less able to identify with Diana's negative feelings concerned with being pushed away from the associate development work.

This gave me the basis of a hypothesis about the degree of unconscious anxiety that the client was carrying, how she was defending against it and how she was unconsciously engaging others in supporting her view of the world. In this case I felt that there was parallel process occurring between the coach and Diana. The coach was matching Diana's response by paying attention to the same things and avoiding confronting the anxiety in relation to the real task challenges.

### Key concept – *parallel process*

'Parallel process' is what happens when what is going on between the coach and his or her client matches or mirrors what the client is doing inside his or her organization.

In this instance, Diana was ignoring her negative emotions and focusing too much on the positive feelings she felt about the task that she enjoyed the most. JD ended up mirroring her positive feelings and excitement in the session and failed to tune in to the negative ones. Parallel process is a powerful lens from the psychodynamic model that enables the coach to quickly enter into the client's inner world, provided that he or she can keep a little part of him or herself alert to this when he or she is in the coaching session.

In relation to the FSM, parallel process links with psychological perspectives as it highlights some of what may be going on unconsciously for the client and possibly the coach. This can raise awareness about blind spots or typical response patterns. In addition, parallel process can help to highlight where the energy in a situation tends to be focused or drained. The insight derived from this can help support more effective energy management as highlighted in the green perspective of the FSM. Furthermore, parallel process takes us into the systemic level of what may be going on for the client. It can illuminate in some fascinating and helpful ways what is playing out in the wider system and is a valuable framework in the systemic perspective of the FSM.

*Supervisor exercise*
*– raising awareness of the parallel process*

1. Is there anything in what or how the coach is depicting the coaching relationship that mirrors any aspect of what the client is dealing with in his or her work situation?

2. What specifically is being mirrored between the coach and the client that reflects the client's issue at work? Is it behaviors? Is it emotions?

3. How aware do you think the coach is of the parallel process? What is your evidence?

4. If you think that you have detected a parallel process, ask the coach, "What parallels can you see between how the client was interacting with you in the coaching session and how the client was dealing with this issue at work?"

5. Help your supervisee explore what this parallel process may mean for the client and what it may mean for the coach themselves.

JD had spent the rest of the session trying to help the client to build the basis of a plan to win more business. This activity, it transpired, was more at JD's initiative than the clients. JD commented on the fact that Diana had seemed rather flat in her responses and that there was no sense of urgency or that she would act upon what they had discussed.

I decided that my task in that moment as a supervisor was to help JD explore his own emotional response to Diana's situation and to investigate and to gain insight into the inconsistencies. I asked JD how he felt about the size of the task facing his client. He paused for a moment and then said actually he felt it was huge and rather daunting. I asked him whether he had picked up at all during the session that the young partner felt it was such. He replied: "No – not really – mild annoyance but she largely seemed to be brushing it aside." This insight then opened up the supervision conversation at a number of levels.

*Key concept –* **the role of the unconscious**

**KEY CONCEPT**

The psychodynamic model assumes that emotions play a much larger role in our behaviors and responses than most people would generally believe. In particular the model says that human beings deal with uncomfortable emotions by pushing them down into the unconscious mind and holding them at bay so they don't feel too frightening or overwhelming. The more positive, easier to deal with emotions tend to be held in the conscious mind. This inevitably leads to a subtle interplay between the conscious and unconscious minds as the negative emotions play up to the surface as events trigger them. This is how the name 'psychodynamic' comes about, from the dynamic interplay between the two parts of the mind.

First, we were able to explore how JD would describe Diana's defenses. JD realized that the feelings of anxiety about not being able to deliver the task were causing the partner to shut down and not be able to think with any degree of clarity about what she needed to do differently. We talked about the sometimes subtle differences between denial and rationalization (more on this in a later case example). I asked JD what he felt the denial was protecting the client from.

JD then began to wonder whether Diana was actually quite angry. He said that he had felt a brief flash of anger as she had described the risk of having her "special project" taken away from her. She had sounded irritated when talking about having to do something she felt she was not good at and did not enjoy. There had also been an edge in her voice when she talked about feeling powerless to challenge the situation.

JD said that when the client had spoken about all of these frustrations in relation to having to focus on the sales task she had fidgeted in quite a tense way and clenched her hands into fists while speaking. But importantly, JD now seemed to be feeling that Diana may actually be unable to acknowledge her own anger in an appropriate way. JD realized that while Diana remained disconnected from the angry part of herself she would be blocked from mobilizing herself to engage with the sales task.

*Key concept –* **the role of anxiety**

**KEY CONCEPT**

The role of anxiety is considered central in the psychodynamic model. Human beings deploy elaborate emotional defensive mechanisms to protect themselves from feelings of anxiety. In this instance, the anxiety about the sales task is stopping the client realize that underneath it all she is really angry. Feeling angry is scary, especially if you like to relate to yourself as a nice, warm person who helps others (as in the case of Diana). While this client remains unaware that she may actually feel very angry about what she is being asked to do, she will never be able to fully engage with the task in hand in a realistic and honest way.

**TIP**

The work of the coach here is to enable the client to look at, accept and integrate the part of him or herself that he or she does not want to admit to – the angry part in this case. It is accepting this angry aspect that is actually making the client anxious. It is the anxiety that is keeping the client blocked and locked out of taking effective action.

All in all, it is quite a complicated circuit of emotions. A psychodynamic approach encourages us not to take what the client brings at face value but rather to look beneath the surface for the conflicting emotions in dynamic tension that may be what is keeping the client stuck.

Understanding the role of anxiety helps us take a deep psychological view of the client through the supervisee's lens. This supports the blue elements of the FSM. Understanding anxiety also links to the 'energy management', 'self-awareness and support' petals of the FSM, the green aspects of the FSM. When the coach can spot and contain his or her own anxiety and that of his or her client then both will be managing their energy much more effectively. A psychodynamic approach can be particularly helpful in this regard.

This important insight, derived from taking a psychodynamic view of the work, highlighted an approach that JD could adopt in the next session to begin to unlock the immobilized state that the client was in. If JD could gently put Diana in touch with just how angry she may be feeling and enable her to start to tolerate these feelings then she would begin to become free of this blockage. This insight enabled JD to start thinking about what he may tackle in the next session.

JD was unsure as to how he may do this. It would be entirely inappropriate and counterproductive to mention any of these issues directly. JD needed to find an everyday way of addressing them. We looked at the 'In your shoes' technique where the coach could start by saying that reflecting on the previous conversation he was left thinking that were he to find himself in a similar situation he thought he would feel really quite upset and angry at having to leave behind work that he loved in order to focus on sales, which was something he did not especially enjoy. This technique normalizes the emotion that the client is struggling to acknowledge and integrate by showing the client that the coach himself/herself may feel that way and that this is OK.

*Key concept – **psychodynamic coaching techniques***

**KEY CONCEPT**

The coach should not (or almost never) set out these psychodynamic concepts directly to the client. Telling a client it is his or her anxiety that is the problem that is blocking him or her from taking effective action is likely to get a pretty negative response.

Instead, the art of using this model in practice is to allow it to inform the coach's thinking and then to apply this in a subtle and everyday way with the client. The technique highlighted above does this.

We then looked at JD's own emotional reaction to the client's response – this is known as 'countertransference'. JD had also played down the difficult feelings. This seemed to be what the client wanted him to do and he had responded accordingly, thus ratifying or colluding with the client's position. He had at one level been unconsciously hooked by the client's desire to seek an ally in her stance. However, when we carried on investigating it also turned out that there was more to it than that and that JD may have a similar blind spot that could make him prone to not reacting to situations that made him angry.

I asked JD about his own experiences within his family in relation to difficult emotions. It turned out that in his family people "did not do anger". They either brushed an issue aside, making light of it, or removed themselves until the worst had passed. We were able to identify that JD was entirely comfortable not confronting angry emotions himself. Thus it had been easy for him to mirror and get caught in the client's pattern in this regard as it matched his own. This was a critical insight. JD would be powerless to help the client unblock his or her anger in a constructive way if this was also a blind spot for himself.

### Key concept – *countertransference*

**KEY CONCEPT**

Countertransference refers to the coach's own emotional reaction to the client. It is important for the coach to have a strong awareness of which feelings that arise during a session come from his or her own past experiences and which feelings are specifically being invoked by this particular client.

JD's feeling of wanting to warmly support and become an ally was an example of his countertransference with this client. In addition, in this instance, these feelings were also a real clue to his own ego defenses and how they created a potential blind spot for him as a coach.

Thus, by exploring the countertransference in this specific instance we found an extremely rich source of data. This data was vital in supporting the coach to do more effective work with the client as well as develop his or her own personal insight.

Countertransference links to several perspectives of the FSM model. We can see its connections to the psychological (blue elements). It also links with 'self-awareness and support' and 'energy management' (the green aspects of FSM). If, as supervisors, we can support the coach to raise his or her awareness around countertransference, the coach will be able to become much more present to the client and the client's emotional inner world. This, in turn, will help to build the relationship and learning environment for the client (the yellow perspective). Finally, paying careful attention to countertransference can also shed light on certain aspects of what may be going on at a systemic level within the client's world (the blue perspective).

*Supervisor exercise –*

**using countertransference to support insight**

In your next supervision session pay particular attention to how the supervisee describes how his or her client left him or her feeling. Here are some examples of the type of questions you may ask the supervisee:

**1.** How did the client leave you feeling when she was discussing a particular issue?

**2.** Was your emotional reaction to the client on this issue one that you recognize in yourself as a common reaction? Or do you feel it was evoked more particularly by the client in relation to the issue she was presenting?

**3.** What may your emotional reaction to the client on this occasion tell you about what is going on for the client?

**4.** What else would you like to explore with the client now, as a result of analyzing your emotional reaction to her on this issue?

In summary, a psychodynamic approach as used in this supervision session provided a very fast track into a number of key and deep-seated issues for both the coach and his client. Each of the lenses used here enabled the coach to learn a lot about himself quickly, to come up with some key hypotheses to work on with the client and a technique for fronting into a complex emotional issue without frightening or closing the client down.

## The unrelentingly driven client

This time we meet Emma, a very experienced coach whose style is quite direct and solution focused. Emma has a reputation for adding value fast to her clients.

This case study explores:

▼ *the defense mechanisms of rationalization and projective identification*

▼ *the role of unconscious patterns from early and past relationships – transference and countertransference – and how these can help the coach to understand the inner world of the client and what keeps him or her stuck in unproductive patterns*

▼ *the coach–client relationship as an important source of insight and as an agent of change – over time enabling the client to acknowledge and accept the less appealing parts of himself/herself so that he or she can better govern his or her own behavior.*

Emma wanted to discuss a long-standing client, Richard, in this session. This was their second coaching program together and Richard had come back into coaching because he had recently been promoted to the position of president of a large division within the pharmaceutical company where he worked. Emma had an established relationship with Richard and quite a lot of information about him and his background, both personal and professional.

Richard had been in the new role for eight months. He had just received 360 feedback from his new leadership team. On the one hand, the team were very positive about his task focus and about his deep knowledge of the sector. (The previous incumbent had been rather distant and laissez faire.) They also really appreciated his readiness to get involved and to help them tackle thorny issues.

On the other hand, they frequently found him too controlling, micromanaging and intense. This manifested in his own intense work rate, his expectation of the team to match it, his demand for huge amounts of data and detail and a constant underlying sense that he was questioning their delivery ability, which raised the question of whether he really trusted them.

Emma had opened the supervision session by saying that she felt rather "stuck" with this client right now, in the sense that she could not seem to get him to engage with the feedback in any meaningful way. This left Emma feeling, "So what I am doing here and what value can I add then?" We started to explore in the supervision session what was incorporated into that feeling of 'stuckness'.

*Key concept – **the role of emotion***

**KEY CONCEPT**

In the psychodynamic approach looking under the surface of the emotions that present in the coach is a key starting point. It would be very easy to start trying to be helpful in finding strategies to help the coach become unstuck. The real insights, however, lie in going deeply into what the stuck feeling is all about. This central focus on the emotion, both the coach's and the client's, is a core underpinning of the psychodynamic perspective. In my experience as a supervisor I have found it to be very often where the biggest breakthroughs lie.

When Emma asked Richard how he felt about the feedback, he immediately responded that he was not surprised by any of it, he had heard these themes before. He said he knew he was a demanding boss and that was how he got results. He felt the division had been massively undermanaged in the recent past and that it was therefore not delivering what it could and what it should. He felt that the team's capability was "OK but not great" and that if he did not lean in and push hard they would simply not achieve their targets.

I asked Emma how she had felt about Richard's response. Emma observed that it seemed that Richard was not really engaging with the feedback and that there was a feeling of "Yes, OK, they would say that, wouldn't they? And so what?" This had left her wondering what to do next in the session.

We started by exploring how Emma thought Richard was defending himself against really engaging in thinking about the feedback. It appeared that Richard was rationalizing. He had a seemingly logical answer for all the difficult aspects of the feedback. This neatly prevented him from having to look at his own leadership style and behaviors and protected him from the inevitable feelings of discomfort that this would induce. It also had the effect of keeping the coach at bay and inhibiting Emma from doing any 'real' work with the client.

## Key concept – *rationalization as a defense mechanism*

**KEY CONCEPT**

Rationalizing is another defense mechanism identified in the psychodynamic model. The person using rationalization seems, on the face of it, to be thinking about the issue or challenge by what he or she says, but actually he or she is not really. He or she defends him or herself from feeling the uncomfortable emotions that the issue would invoke by coming in quickly with logic and reasons why.

In this case Richard rationalizes by saying that he has to drive and push as the team would not deliver without this. He does not engage with the effect that he has on people. This prevents the coach from getting any purchase on the issue with the client.

Richard had swiftly moved the conversation on from the feedback to complaining about his new boss, the CEO. He recounted how demanding the new boss was, driving relentlessly on increasing the financials all the time. He also mentioned how, in the six months since the new CEO had been in place, not once had he given Richard any positive feedback nor had a proper conversation with him about his ambitions within his role. Richard was really upset and quite angry at the boss's treatment of him.

He gave several examples of how hard he was working to keep the new boss fully in the picture with all the work going on in his division and about how excessively carefully he prepared for board meetings and yet he felt that his business results and his performance in the boardroom went unacknowledged. Richard said that he felt that nothing ever felt good enough for the new boss.

I asked Emma if she could see any connections or similarities between these two elements of the dialog with Richard. She thought for a moment and then observed that there were a couple of key similarities. First, Richard in both scenarios was 'filling the space' with lots of information and lots of detail, leaving nothing to chance or open discussion. Second, the feeling that the team was left with by Richard and the feeling that Richard was left with by his boss were similar. Namely they felt both "controlled" and "under-appreciated". Emma observed that there appeared to be a parallel process occurring whereby what Richard was doing to his direct reports was what his boss was doing to him.

### Key concept – *parallel process*

As both a coach and a supervisor it pays to listen carefully for parallel process (described above). When it occurs, it can provide huge clues as to what the client's inner world looks like and what his or her deeply held habitual patterns may be.

In this instance, there is a clear pattern emerging in relation to Richard's relationship with authority: how he takes his authority – overly controlling – and how he behaves toward authority – always seeking approval. These are two sides of the same emotional coin. These patterns will come from the early relationships in Richard's life combined with his innate personality. The impact of them is limiting his capacity as a leader. This is one of the key developmental goals for the coach to work on with Richard.

I asked Emma how she had been left feeling during this last session with Richard. Her reply was "de-skilled and like I could not really add much value". Normally she felt they had much more productive, engaged conversations in their session. I suggested that this may be a case of projective identification whereby Richard had unconsciously left Emma feeling exactly like he currently did vis-à-vis the boss – rather useless and not much appreciated. This is another form of defense mechanism designed to prevent the person from actually looking at these difficult feelings in himself/herself.

*Key concept*
## – *projective identification as a defense mechanism*

**KEY CONCEPT**

Projective identification is another form of defense mechanism. Projective identification is subtle and occurs when the client projects his or her unwanted feelings on to the coach and leaves the coach feeling the way that the client does. The client is not able to deal with the difficult emotions, which is why they are projected on to someone else. It is an enormously valuable piece of data for the coach to work with. It requires the coach to keep a little part of him or herself aware of his or her own reactions to the client and not to take these reactions at face value. Yet again we see how in the psychodynamic approach not taking emotions or what is said at face value but staying aware of what may be going on beneath the surface is critically important.

Having identified just how defensive Richard seemed to be at the current time Emma commented on just how anxious and pressured Richard must be feeling. She remarked that she actually felt sorry for him rather than annoyed and frustrated with him.

Emma had successfully used her observation of the defense mechanisms and parallel process to get a much clearer picture of Richard's emotional inner world at the current time. This had enabled her to soften from a place of frustration and she had regained her power as a coach in terms of spotting themes that she could usefully explore with this client to help him move forward.

One of the key themes that she decided she wanted to pick up was around Richard's compulsive 'filling of the space' with mountains of information and his constant over-preparing for meetings and coming across as having all the answers.

I asked whether there was anything that came to mind from Richard's past that may shed light on this pattern. Emma reflected for a while and then said that actually she could see a connection. Richard was the younger of two siblings and his experience growing up was that his parents, in particular his father, favored the older sister. His father had always been quite critical of whatever Richard achieved. If he had done well in exams (which he had) the father would always ask, "Who came top then?" Even when he had had a good grade he never felt that his father was proud of him.

Emma could really see how Richard in his relationship with his boss was constantly pushing for some kind of recognition and approval. His way of doing this (having all the answers) meant that he was actually precluding people from being able to contribute to his thinking and debate and exchange ideas with him. This is a similar pattern to the one he applies to his employees. This is transference in action in the way that Richard is replaying the dynamic between himself and his father.

*Key concept –* **the role of early relationships**

The psychodynamic approach states that our early relationships are of critical importance in creating the behavioral and emotional patterns that we rerun over and over again as adults. This is known as transference. The coach or supervisor using the psychodynamic in his or her work does not need to be a trained therapist or counselor to use these concepts in his or her work.

Helping the supervisee explore and understand the client's early relationships and the way that these may shed light on the current work-related ones can be immensely valuable in: developing self-awareness, deepening the psychological perspective of the work, strengthening the ability to form more effective relationships, understanding what may be playing out systemically, as well as better managing energy. Working in an appropriate way with understanding early relationships is something that a psychodynamic approach holds to be central. As such, this aspect of the psychodynamic touches deeply on the blue, green and yellow elements of the FSM.

*Supervisor exercise –* **use of early relationships to better understand the client in role**

Ask your supervisee what he or she knows of the client's background. If he or she does not have any idea at all then this is interesting data for you as supervisor. You can explore whether he or she had thought about finding out about this. What has stopped him or her? How does he or she feel about asking more about the client's younger days growing up? If he or she is uncomfortable about this, help him or her think about what this discomfort may be about.

Explore with him or her what may be appropriate ways for him or her to ask about the client's personal background and childhood experiences. Help him or her to find a set of questions that he or she will feel comfortable using with his or her client to gain data on the client's early relationships. This is an important area with a psychodynamic approach. Understanding our early relationships helps us to understand our present ones.

**TIP**

> If you are not comfortable yourself as a supervisor in this respect this could be something very helpful to take to your own supervision first before you start working with your own clients in this way.

Emma decided that she would use her own experience of Richard in the last session to open the next one. This would enable them to explore what it felt like to be on the receiving end of being 'blocked out' based on Emma's own experience. This would link back directly to the feedback from the team. Emma would need to handle this especially sensitively. She felt she had sufficient trust in the relationship to do this.

Emma reported back in a future session that this approach had worked with Richard. This client was a particularly data-driven man and the fact that Emma had used real data based on her own experience from the last session had him pay attention. Through questioning, Emma was able to get Richard to link what had happened in the coaching to how Richard's team often felt. This led on to a conversation about how Richard felt when, in his terms, he was "out of control" and did not have the answers.

*Key concept –*
## the client–coach relationship as a source of insight

Emma had skillfully leveraged her relationship with Richard to give the client the experience of the impact that his behavior was having on others. This use of the relationship really helped Richard learn at an experiential level and took him away from his normal defense of rationalizing. This was a pivotal moment in the work and led to Richard being able to open up in a much more flexible and non-controlling way to his colleagues.

Emma took soundings from Richard's team a few weeks after this session and real, tangible behavioral improvements were reported with Richard's team feeling much more motivated.

**Psychodynamic theory:** *some key concepts to remember*

▼ *The role of the emotions is central and greater than is normally thought.*

▼ *Uncomfortable emotions are pushed down into the unconscious mind.*

▼ *Anxiety is an emotion that plays a much greater role than most people are aware of.*

▼ *Human beings use a variety of defense mechanisms to protect themselves against having to really deal with these uncomfortable emotions – notably defense against anxiety.*

▼ *Some of these defense mechanisms are: denial, rationalization, projective identification and idealization. There are other important defenses that it is helpful to know about and understand.*

▼ There is a dynamic tension and interplay between the consciously and unconsciously held emotions. These will play out in a way that it is helpful to pay attention to as a coach and as a supervisor. One such way is parallel process.

▼ The patterns of behavior that we develop early in life in relation to our key care-givers are important. They are embedded patterns that we will replay in key relationships as adults. At work this is often in relation to our superiors. The psychodynamic concept to describe this is 'transference'.

▼ All of the above combine to give rich insight into the client's inner emotional world.

▼ The psychodynamic holds that it is important not to take what the client says or how he or she reacts at face value. The psychodynamic constantly encourages us to look beneath the surface for clues as to the hidden emotional dynamics.

▼ You don't have to be therapeutically trained to make effective use of psychodynamic concepts in coaching or coaching supervision. You just need to be a mindful, reflective practitioner who can apply the principles with tact and skill.

These case studies demonstrate how using the psychodynamic approach in coaching supervision can support the supervisor to enable a level of insight for the coach quickly. This is in the service of the client, helping the work to focus on the critical, often largely subconscious, patterns that need adjusting in order to arrive at the heart of the issue and create lasting behavioral change. There is clearly much more to a psychodynamic approach than one can illustrate in two case studies. I hope, however, that I have been able to introduce you to some of the essence of the thinking in a psychodynamic perspective, as well as demonstrate the immense benefit it can provide in working quickly and deeply with both the supervisee and the client. It is a rich and interesting approach and I hope that many of you will be interested to explore it further.

## FURTHER READING

**Bluckert, Peter (2006)** *Psychological Dimensions of Executive Coaching*, Maidenhead, UK, Open University Press.

**Brunning, Halina (ed.) (2006)** *Executive Coaching: Systems Psychodynamic Perspective,* London: Karnac Books.

**Hawkins, P and Smith, N, (2006)** *Coaching, Mentoring and Organizational Consultancy: Supervision and Development,* Maidenhead, UK: Open University Press.

**Hay, Julie (2007)** *Reflective Practice and Supervision for Coaches,* Maidenhead, UK: Open University Press.

**Hirshhorn, Larry (1990)** *The Workplace Within Psychodynamics of Organizational Life,* London and Cambridge, MA, US: The MIT Press.

**Sandler, Catherine (2011)** *Executive Coaching: A Psychodynamic Approach,* Maidenhead, UK: Open University Press.

# 7 | *Invitation to the music - the transpersonal note in coaching supervision*

## The invitation and the music

THIS CHAPTER is called 'invitation to the music' because it is about a way of fine-tuning our ability as supervisors to pick up the unique 'note' of our supervisee's full self (see the glossary). That note is like having an imaginary tuning fork within us. We hear something that deeply resonates. When that happens, our supervisee also knows that he or she has connected to a place of knowing beyond everyday information, valuable as that is.

The note of the supervisee's full self may even transcend everything already known, giving an extra 'ah-ha' moment sounding from the very core of his or her being. It hugely increases his or her capacity for learning in supervision.

In his 2006 BBC Reith Lectures, Daniel Barenboim said that music takes us to places no other mode of expression can do. The music we listen for in coaching supervision – from a transpersonal perspective – can also take supervisor and supervisee to places that can surprise and amaze us. Hearing this note is encouraged with questions that help tune into that inner ear:

These kinds of questions help us to hear the note:

▼ *What part of this person is speaking to us?*

▼ *How old is that voice?*

▼ *What is emerging in this moment of ambiguity?*

▼ *What truth have you lost sight of?*

▼ *May we stay with that for just a moment and listen for more?*

What is also true is that the silence between the notes in music is just as important as the notes themselves. The essential is that we have created a space and the conditions to listen in a different way. When we do so, we can come to know more than we can know from cognition or emotion alone.

## What bonus does it offer the supervisee?

Developing other ways to know contributes to the development of the 'internal supervisor', the idea that a supervisee begins to build his or her reflective practice, inside himself/herself, becoming more mindfully aware. Drawing upon this inner wisdom he or she can tune into his or her entire range of body, mind, feelings and intuition during each coaching moment.

The transpersonal is a way to deepen discovery and inquiry in the journey of supporting and resourcing coaches in their experience of supervision.

## GLOSSARY

**'Archetype'** – (in Jungian psychology) a collectively inherited unconscious idea, pattern of thought, image, etc, universally present in individual psyches. 'Gestalt' – the theory or doctrine that physiological or psychological phenomena do not occur through the summation of individual elements, as reflexes or sensations, but through gestalts functioning separately or inter-relatedly.

**'Higher self'** – within every person is the 'seed' of this higher self and all that it may become – all of our potential up to and including the notion of the divine spark within us. It is at the core of what motivates and co-ordinates who we are.

**'Namaste'** – a friendly greeting or salutation acknowledging the soul in one person by the soul in the other. It is Asian in origin and is used in some yoga practices.

**'Soul'** – the principle of life, feeling, thought, and action in humans, regarded as a distinct entity separate from the body, and commonly held to be separable in existence from the body; the spiritual part of humans as distinct from the physical part.

**'Temenos'** – from the Greek, meaning 'sacred enclosure'.

**'Transpersonal'**– the word 'transpersonal' has become an umbrella term for naming that experience where consciousness extends beyond (trans) the individual or personal ego and the everyday journey of life.

**'Transcendence'** – one way of looking at transcendence is when the quality of what emerges when thinking can go beyond, for example, two quite different mindsets or 'positions' and bring with it a sense of transformation that is more than the sum of its individual parts.

**'Wise, compassionate observer'** – an unconditional kindliness towards ourselves that is without judgment.

## What do we really mean by 'transpersonal'?

The word 'transpersonal' has become an umbrella term for naming that experience where consciousness extends beyond (trans) the individual or personal ego and the everyday journey of life. For many it carries a spiritual dimension characterized by a sense of inner peace, compassion for others, reverence for life, gratitude and appreciation both for unity and diversity.

Transpersonal psychology emerged in California in the late 1960s through a group of men and women that included William James, Carl Jung, Roberto Assagioli and Abraham Maslow, among others. They were interested in the empirical, scientific study of inner states of consciousness. These pioneers wanted to honor the experience of states of mind not being recognized by other approaches to psychological thinking.

The birth of the transpersonal, as distinct and different from other approaches in psychology, was marked by the first issue of the *Journal of Transpersonal Psychology* (1969). In the UK, three centers representing transpersonal psychology in the early 1970s were established.

## What does it mean to experience the transpersonal?

Experiencing the transpersonal dimension can be described as inhabiting the wider spaces within one's being.

Unlike many other psychological perspectives it is not a pathological one. This means that the focus is on the part of us that is whole, free and fully alive within us; this helps us work with our limitations and challenges and be the best that we can be.

This perspective aligns so clearly with the ethos of coaching, which focuses on potential and seeks out the positive in order to go forward.

Many of our coaches say that it is felt in moments they become aware of a greater sense of themselves.

## Try this:

Can you think of a time when you have been deeply moved by a piece of music or a poem? Have you ever had an 'ah-ha' experience when the hairs on the back of your neck stood up?

The transpersonal can often be felt when, even fleetingly, we have a sense of meaning and connection to something larger than ourselves. This kind of transpersonal awareness includes all of our ordinary waking states *plus* higher states of awe, bliss and deep calm. This dimension is part of each person who sits with a coach or a supervisor.

Current neuroscience offers much research to suggest that resting in spacious awareness, these additional states allow one to access a greater inner resource for understanding, insight and wisdom (Hanson, 2009). This is true in the adult learning space of coaching supervision.

## How does this apply to coaching supervision?

Working in this way, a supervisor meets his or her supervisee at the interface between the outer world with all its demands of the here and now, and the internal world of the individual, rich with symbols, stories, even dreams. If we listen for the music behind and underneath the conversation we can be open to honoring a much wider field of possibility. The transpersonal is not a single model. It is a lens or a perspective on seeing life – personal, professional and business life. Whatever maps, frameworks or models a coach or supervisor already is familiar with need not be surrendered. Instead, a transpersonal perspective colors the way the frameworks and models may be seen, felt and experienced.

Many coaches are familiar with the importance of a 'shift' in thinking within a coaching session. A transpersonal shift comes from an awakening of knowledge within us that is sometimes felt as 'more'. We are aware of more of ourselves. Some would say that this aspect called 'more' was always there but we have been cut off from parts of ourselves – often for many historically rooted reasons. In some senses we are retrieving what was already ours which, for whatever reasons, was not accessible to us.

In terms of the Full Spectrum Model, the transpersonal is like a gossamer net that holds and contains the whole model and everything beyond. This numinous and ephemeral 'net' gives us a panoramic gaze that includes all aspects of the Model plus the higher consciousness. It is informed by the collective field, archetypes and ancestors, eastern and western traditions of knowing, as well as the mysteries of not knowing. This additional field is at our disposal to inform, stimulate and guide us. It is the soul and spirit of inquiry during supervision sessions. It enhances both the supervisor and the supervisee's capacity for true learning by awakening true compassion that is mindful, clear and loving.

> *"When there is no space the eternal cannot visit,*
> *when there is no space, the soul cannot awaken."*
>
> - O'Donohue, 1999

**CASE STUDY 1**

In one particular supervision session a supervisee brought an issue about a final session with one of his clients. The client had repeatedly postponed the session, often with little notice. My supervisee could not understand why he was so nonplussed about this when he knows that he should have stronger feelings. He said he felt nothing at all. I asked him, in a very gentle way, what endings were like for him. "Ah," he said, "my father left our family three times before I was 13. After the third time he never returned. I just cut myself off from having any expectations." We sat in the stillness after he finished speaking. Almost a minute passed where neither of us spoke. "I shut down first," he said quietly. "If there is a chance of being left, I shut down first."

"Mmmm," I said, and we sat for a few more seconds. "That's what is influencing me here, again, even though it is a different time and place," he realized. "I need to call and speak to my client. Now I know that I can come from the right place inside me to do that."

My role as supervisor was simply to hold the invitational space. My supervisee could listen a bit deeper to what was emerging and could honor that piece of history and its impact. He could tune into his own insight a bit more each time, appreciating the wider range of factors at play within himself.

### Starting with the supervisor

What is certainly true is that for the transpersonal to be useful in a coaching supervision session, supervisors must authentically be available to the notion of the transpersonal in themselves. It then comes from the heart and soul. To work in this way, the supervisor must be willing to step into this space himself/herself.

And so, we honor the uniqueness of the supervisee and attend with all the skills and dimensions of supervision, which we are clearly outlined in the Full Spectrum Model. In these difficult times there is so much uncertainty and stress, the transpersonal is particularly helpful. We listen for that note of the deeper and wider field that underpins all. It brings a kind of grace in the supervision dialog even when the conversations are provocative. By being open to this perspective we can become available to a higher or deeper state of consciousness rich in wisdom and articulated at a soulful level. This openness, of course, is the invitation to our own music, too.

**CASE STUDY 2**

I was working with an internal coach I'll call Gary, who was coaching a senior civil servant. He was feeling more and more deskilled as the work with his client became more erratic each time they met. Actions identified as vital were shelved on each subsequent coaching session. There seemed to be no firm ground to stand on. Everything was shifting. "I'm not sure how I am being useful to this person," Gary said. The nature of the work his client was involved in indicated that this changeability was a 'normal' state of affairs. I asked Gary if he had felt like this before. He said he did when he first joined the internal coaching team. "What did you call upon in yourself to help you then, given that you had less experience than you do now?" I asked. Gary sat for a while but he said he just didn't know.

I then asked, "If a wise part of you was standing here now reviewing what you do as a coach, what non-judgmental and kindly advice would you get?" After a while Gary said, "Back then I wasn't so porous. I was able to ask my clients to stop and reflect more, to step away from the endless 'it's-never-good-enough' feeling that permeates the whole department and to just breathe and take stock. I used to do that for me too. I think we both need that back."

Inviting that wise, compassionate part of ourselves into the supervision conversation can provide a bit more space to be more deeply aware of what information is available in the vast, wise resource within.

By using the 'wise, compassionate observer', the learning space in coaching supervision takes on a real sense of the 'super' in our vision as supervisor and supervisee work together. The physicist, David Bohm (1980) writes of an "implicate order" – a deeper level of reality that exists beyond anything we can articulate, a dimension where everything is connected to everything. Such a shift in thinking helps us understand how collective alignment happens between people. Collective alignment describes what happens when, for example, people in a group start to function as a whole ensemble, like a jazz group or a championship rowing crew.

## Three transpersonal concepts and their application in supervision

### The concept of the journey of the two selves

In transpersonal psychology we speak of a variety of meanings clustered around the word 'self'. Philosophically, at the heart of this way of working is a belief that there is a spark within each one of us – in our core – that is whole and eternal. One way to look at this is through the concept of two journeys a person makes in his or her life. One 'self' (designated by a small 's') means the total person, including the persona, the ego and the unconscious. This is the everyday self with all the attendant issues of work, career and kids, challenges that we experience in our lives and that, as coaches and supervisors, we are accustomed to encountering.

Different from that, but also on the journey through life, is the Self with a large 'S'. This designates the second meaning – the higher Self. Within every person is the 'seed' of this higher Self and all that it may become – all of our potential up to and including the notion of the divine spark within us. It is at the core of what motivates and co-ordinates who we are. It is a wise core that, whatever our difficulties in the everyday world we live in, there is a connection to this Self within us. It is always there for us to access if we wish. Its purpose is to seek meaning in life and act as a balancing force within us to reach our potential. Our connection to this helps renew us in profound and deep ways. It may have something to tell us. It may arrive when we least expect or welcome it.

For example, in the midst of a coaching supervision session my supervisee began to talk quite passionately about the impact of huge changes in the life of her client. She listed energetically to all the hurdles her client faced and how she felt for her client's distress. Now and again she would tap a finger on her chest, almost imperceptivity. After some time I drew her attention to this gesture. "Can I ask what that hand is saying?" She stopped in mid-sentence. She seemed almost shocked.

"That," she said finally, "is 'me'. *Where am I in this?* I am losing myself and my needs in selling the changes here in our company. *What about me*, is what it is saying. *What about me?*"

Our higher Self can offer a reservoir of insight, compassion and wisdom that is as old as us, if not older. This part manifests within us in the crises and experiences, both high and low, of human living. It is the part of us that 'knows' what, in our heart of hearts, is our truth, our unique note.

## Try this reflective activity now:

Think of a time when you may have had a transpersonal experience – something that really touched or moved you or you had a spiritual awakening.

Allow the question to sit with you, or even sleep on it, and see what may arise the day after.

Write down the qualities that made up that experience and how you felt about yourself in the moment.

Where are those moments in your life now?

## The concept of the 'wise, compassionate observer'

The wise, compassionate observer is within each of us. It is an unconditional kindliness toward ourselves that is without judgment. Buddhists call this '*maitri*'. It encourages us to take a moment to see the whole, including ourselves, with compassion and to understand this 'whole' without reducing it or only criticizing it – of ourselves or others. In a world where so much is seen as dualistic – as good or bad, as right or wrong – this is a place to be – however briefly – that is free from the tension of 'it-must-be-this-or-it-must-be-that', of polarized thinking. It gives us an opportunity to refresh what we really know and to not be snagged wholly by the power of the 'inner critic'.

The wise, compassionate observer is not about platitudes. It does not replace all the fine work the supervisor and supervisee would normally do. It may well say:

▼ *Well it hasn't gone quite like you wished, what else can you see at play here?*

▼ *What do you know but have forgotten?*

▼ *What part of you is responding in this way?*

▼ *Who are you for this person?*

▼ *What treasure can be redeemed?*

▼ *What is calling for deeper attention – a wiser eye?*

▼ *What understanding is emerging?*

**TIP**

Try this before you begin a session:

▼ *As you prepare yourself to begin a supervision session, and before your supervisee arrives, take a few minutes to check in with yourself.*

▼ *Close your eyes. Invite the wise, compassionate observer in you to join in the space with grace, compassion and love.*

▼ *Connect to your soul self in whatever way feels right to you, as you sit in the chair.*

▼ *Take a deep breath and settle into alert awareness.*

*The concept of the coaching supervision space as sacred – a* **temenos**

We call the space we work in a '*temenos*', from the Greek meaning 'sacred enclosure'. Whether a supervisor has a spiritual practice or not, we see the space in which we sit together as being like a mirrored bowl. In this space we both are visible. In the beginning of a session, we are ready for the work and are also silently inviting the soul or spirit, call it what you will, of the work to join us.

We need to come with compassion for this bigger space in ourselves, for the best in ourselves to show up as supervisors. We hold that space for others too, even when it is not named explicitly. Martin Buber describes what we bring in ourselves to the "I and thou" space between supervisor and supervisee, "as reclaiming the consciousness of our essential, inherent and original wholeness and embracing our fragmentation" (Buber, 1971). In this perspective we know that the relational space, between the 'I and thou', constitutes the web of life. It allows us to break free from the 'known' and move into the opening and unfolding of the mystery of life.

## Mid-life change and challenges

Another way a transpersonal perspective can be very helpful in coaching supervision is supporting coaches working with clients facing mid-life change. At this juncture clients often bring issues where the path in their life is no longer as clear as it seemed to be before. Strong competing demands on their time and their lives are different. Confusion arrives because old solutions no longer work.

In transpersonal psychology we would say it is at this point in personal development, whatever age the person is, when the ego begins to move more towards being in service to the higher Self, rather than the other way around. Wanting to serve a greater good, discover or revive old interests, giving back, going deeper – these are some elements that emerge in mid-life coaching. It may be a yearning for a more soulful or spiritual connection in life. Discovering and living aspects of unlived life may come pushing from somewhere inside to be heard, seen and counted (Edinger, 1972).

Coaching clients often bring issues that are wider and more searching than the job or the promotion alone. They may seek a role for themselves that is not solely in service to the organization's, or others', needs and goals. They want work that will satisfy something more than that. Some of the executives we coach will want their coach to explore issues about meaning in their working and personal lives, about who they are and about the journey of life itself.

For example:

▼ *the chairperson who has no position 'higher' to go in his or her organization other than out, but still has more to give*

▼ *an unexpected redundancy at 56*

▼ *a highly desired retirement now indefinitely delayed*

▼ *what seemed a 'prize role' begins to feel hollow*

▼ *a relationship ends after decades together*

Sometimes the way forward is not clear for a client. This 'not knowing' is an important stage and from it many people redesign their life, reconfirm their values and find fresh or long-lost paths. Becoming more comfortable with ambiguity may be a characteristic of the terrain. Many life and business coaches – as well as coach supervisors – work with these features of life every day.

In supervision some questions our supervisees arrive with are:

▼ *How can I help my client hold something that feels so nameless at the moment, especially when I am so much younger than he is?*

▼ *What can I do to best support my client find her dream and yet serve the system we both are a part of?*

▼ *How can we explore the creative flow my client feels he has lost?*

▼ *What sorts of things could I bring to my coaching that would be more creative than currently?*

▼ *They are making my client redundant after 25 years. How can I help my client with her sadness and her anger?*

▼ *How can I support my client as he responds to what his heart wants him to do?*

These are big challenges to an individual and an organization. Sometimes supervisees can feel a little uprooted in their confidence or skills. This calls upon the supervisor to bring a greater depth of presence and a larger container for the breadth of the supervision conversation. In this wide change agenda, supporting coaches to feel personally resourced is a vital part of what supervision can offer on this journey – however bumpy it may be at times and however much inquiry, transition, grace, creativity and meaning it holds.

**TIP**

Try these questions:

▼ *Where do you draw your inspiration from?*

▼ *When you have been in a tight corner what gets you going again?*

▼ *What strength has brought you through those changes?*

▼ *What is evoked when you hear yourself say that?*

▼ *Can you allow an image to arise for how that was for you?*

▼ *What part of you is summoning this change of direction?*

▼ *What makes your heart sing?*

## Three ways to work from this perspective: visualization, drawing and the Magic Box

The following are ways to work with and incorporate a transpersonal note in the supervision conversation.

### Guided imagery exercises

As long as humankind has existed it has made and used symbols. Symbols can provide a common language. They often strengthen the bridge between the inner and outer worlds, bringing richness. Guided exercises can help the supervisee move from a purely 'head' response to responding from other parts of themselves that 'know'. This helps him or her gain even more insight. Some exercises simply ask the person to find an image in his or her mind's eye. Others are guided visualizations, often short, which invite the person into a described scene. They can be used as part or all of a supervision session. I use a variety of different ones. Silverstone (1997) is a great resource.

*How to try this out*

Make sure you have enough time to do an exercise and debrief it. Invite the supervisees to make themselves comfortable and to close their eyes to help reduce or eliminate distractions around them. Be sure you are somewhere that will allow you to do this safely and where you will not be uninterrupted. Ask them for the duration of the exercise to suspend any self-judging voice that may interfere with unhelpful thoughts like, "Nothing is coming," "What if I don't get a good (enough) image?" and "I missed that part" It doesn't matter. Whatever comes up as he or she goes through the guided exercise the outcome will be valuable for discussion.

Have some blank paper and colored pencils handy so there is an option to capture the essence of the exercise as soon as you finish and before you discuss it. Drawing helps to ground the image in the here and now and have it available for possible further reference. Even rudimentary recording often adds information that illuminates the story the supervisee tells you. You can use this exercise at any point that feels appropriate in a session. In my experience the image that arises will always have value for the person drawing it.

CASE STUDY 3

### Using imagery and drawing

My supervisee, Sophie, and I worked together by distance using Skype. Sophie is a coach at the head office of a Danish public sector organization. She said that she felt less confident, particularly around the most senior staff. "My client seems so much larger than life, like a large ship coming into port," she explained. When she began to think like that she didn't feel she did her best.

I asked her if we could try a creative approach to explore this. I asked her that if the client seemed like a large ship, what kind of boat was she and asked her if she would be willing to draw it on some paper. The picture she showed me was of a small brown row boat with a single oar. She said she felt that as soon as she saw herself as small she started going in circles in a session.

I then asked her that if her most wise self were to draw a boat that reflected how she was as a coach what it would be like. She said, "It would draw a tug boat." She said that big ships are too large to get right into the shore while a tug boat is nimble and quick and that tugs provide a very important service.

After some time she held up a second picture with colors and some kind of equipment on the back of it. It was much bolder. She said she knew that if she had her heart in the right place, she recognized her value and was much more focused. If she saw solely the "bigness" of the client then she lost sight of herself. For Sophie, she said, the drawing took her to a deeper understanding quicker than just talking about it. She felt remembering it would help her get the right balance.

## Magic Box

The 'Magic Box' originates from both Sandplay and Gestalt practice. In this version we use a box of three-dimensional objects of any kind (such as figures, stones, shells or toys) for the supervisee (or coach) to choose from so that the imaginative and creative part of the self can operate outside the confines of the analytic mind. In this way, supervisees can be playful as well as creative in the service of their learning. It's called "Magic" because of the high value that comes from using this box of objects to tell a story about what may be going on in a given situation – and because what emerges may be so unexpected and helpful.

In this way of working the supervisee chooses as many objects as needed to represent a system or situation to be explored. The story is discussed as the picture is built. Some of the objects may change place if the supervisee wants to 'try out' a new perspective, allowing some fluidity in seeing or being with the situation. The Magic Box can be used to explore ideas as well as concrete situations from multiple perspectives. See the end of this chapter for guidelines on using this way of working.

**TIP**

### Inside the Magic Box

Use the language of the space and the objects during the whole exercise.

Debrief the activity as a whole only when all of the activity in the 'scene' is finished.

**CASE STUDY 4**

### Magic Box

Supervisee Joanne was coaching a vice principal in a large further education college. The result of the coaching so far was causing no small amount of turmoil as the confidence of the client was growing. The chair of governors and the management team was happy at first with the work that Joanne was doing but were now getting worried about the reverberations. The coaching contract was indeed about having impact across the senior team and beyond. The supervisee didn't want to fall from favor with the college. On the other hand, she wanted to serve her coachee's needs. She felt a bit stuck. I suggested we try a different approach.

From a large basket with random items of stones, shells, small action figures and other objects I asked her to select an item that represented herself and to place it on the piece of cloth (forming the 'stage') where we were going to represent her supervision issue (see Figure 7.1).

**K:** *Joanne, can you please place the object that represents yourself wherever you feel is right. And then tell me why you picked that item and that place on the cloth to put it.*

**J:** *I am on the right-hand edge because I feel I might be going out the door if this doesn't work. I picked this shell because it is like one of those larger ones that when you hold it to your ear you hear the sea. I think I am a good listener and yet I am very contained.*

**K:** *Can you now pick something that represents your client and tell me a little about that?*

**J:** *This is TinTin and I have placed him in the middle of the space. He has positioned himself right in the center of things and he's really eager to get stuck into making changes in his role in the SMT [Senior Management Team] but the principal seems to never be around to support him in front of the others, though he says privately that's what he wants.*

**K:** *OK, would it be good to pick something that stands for the Principal, if that feels right? (This time she picked a tiny painted box in which were four minute stick 'worry' figures.)*

**J:**  *I never know who I am getting with him, he is so changeable –
he's all these different people and one of them is always
worrying. I have known him and worked with the college for
five years and he has always been that way. (She places the
little box in another corner of the space with only one of the
figures left beside it.)*

**K:**  **Are there any other people that needed to be
represented in the scene?**

**J:**  *Yes, the finance director – he's a spider sitting just outside the
scene in the top right corner and here are a few marbles to
stand for a number of heads of departments that are
uncertain what their roles will be going forward with
the reorganization and are pushing backup to the Senior
Management Team (SMT). That's it, I think.*

**K:**  **What do you make of this picture? What are you
curious about?**

**J:**  *Everyone is so far apart. There is no connection with the
needs and concerns of all these parties. Everyone is
disconnected. I feel disconnected just looking at it. TinTin is
facing away from his team. Even though he is trying to get
them to see things differently they can't see him really – which
is true. I hadn't really appreciated that. As it's a multisite
college they are not all in the same building every day anyway.*

**K:**  **TinTin usually has a dog, doesn't he? Dogs are often
associated with our instinctive self – so where's his
intuition in the midst of change?**

**J:**  *He is developing his communication skills but he isn't
recognizing own impact. He isn't reading the space from others'
perspectives – a bit too gung-ho, like a TinTin.*

She dived into the box to add a small object to stand for his intuition
and turn the figure around to face the heads of departments
(marbles), the finance director and the principal. She moved the

small box to place it a bit closer to the other and took out the remaining tiny figures.

**J:** *I also need to explore how he can work with the different sides of the principal. I also need to remember the principal, after knowing my work for the last five years, has confidence in me.*

**K:** **What about the marbles, they seem to still be rolling about…?**

**J:** *As soon as one stops another rolls away. The heads need some sense of containment (and picked some more things from the basket to create that container). With the role my client is taking up, the principal needs to encourage more middle management leadership in each curriculum area to help them be more effective.*

**K:** *And the spider?*

**J:** *Oh, the spider is OK actually. He just needs more concrete clarity from each area that all is OK and the budget is adhered to. Oh, and I think I have to come out of my shell more and offer more in-the-moment feedback that could help my coachee understand what it's like to be working with him. He has asked me for that and so far I have not done it enough.*

We debriefed what Joanne got from this 'Magic Box' exercise. She said one of the most important things was to come out of her head and use more of herself to understand the dynamics at play. It seemed like completely random objects but they really told a story. "It has helped me to tune in and see the bigger picture. Everything I picked resonated in some way with what is happening in my client's world. It has helped me see the system and the players, symbolically and in reality."

**Figure 7.1** - *Placement of objects to represent a supervision issue*

Be curious – stay within the spirit of the scene:

▼ *What does it look like from here? There?*

▼ *What do you think about the space between the figures?*

▼ *What is happening between these figures?*

▼ *What would it be like if you moved?*

▼ *What would it be like if they moved?*

▼ *What would it be like if no-one moved?*

Cognition and rational decision-making skills are highly prized by clients, sponsors and organizations. However, we can easily lose sight of the other ways that we can 'know' and understand the dynamics at play within and between people. As Einstein said, "The problems of today will never be solved at the same level of thinking that created them." The transpersonal is a way to deepen discovery and inquiry in the journey of supporting and resourcing coaches in their experience of supervision.

By being open to this perspective ourselves we serve our supervisees by helping them tap into and trust that there is a part of them rich in wisdom, articulated at a soulful level right here at hand within us. This openness is the invitation to listen out for that unique note that may arise and inform us from our heart and our soul as coach supervisors.

"[F]or those who have matured to a responsible, stable ego, the next stage of growth is the beginning of the transpersonal, the level of psychic intuition, of transcendent openness and clarity, the awakening that is somehow more than the simple mind and body."

**Wilbur cited in Vaughn, 1986: 214**

## Footnote

The work described in this chapter does not necessarily replace a deeper exploration that may be more appropriate in a psychotherapeutic setting. This may be an appropriate referral, in line with being clear about boundaries, contracts and awareness of the competency of a coach or of a supervisor. This would no doubt be something to discuss in supervision itself.

**Added resource 1:** *guided visualization: the magic gift shop*

Imagine yourself on a street in a town anywhere in the world... (Pause) Follow this road through your curiosity until you come to a little street that is very narrow... (Pause)

Walk down this street and see many shops and cafes in different colors... (Pause) Explore this street, taking in all the sights, sounds, colors and smells as you explore... (Pause)

You come to a gift shop and you are very interested in entering it. It is full to the top with so many different things from many places. Take time to walk through this shop and look at all the wonderful things inside. You can pick up and touch anything in the shop. Notice the things that you are drawn to... (Pause)

When you have explored the whole shop the owner says that you may choose one gift to take away with you... Take some time in selecting just the right gift to take with you... (Pause) When you have chosen, thank the shop owner and leave the shop... Make your way down the little street... (Pause)

Turn into the road where you began your exploration and with your gift return to the present moment here in this room.

**Silverstone (1997).**
Reproduced with permission of Jessica Kingsley Publishers.

**Added resource 2:** *how to use the Magic Box*

1. Any kind of small objects will work because it is not what they are but what they may represent symbolically. Easily portable items are good if you are working peripatetically. Use your imagination and enjoy collecting them. Even a bag of very varied buttons works well and they are light to carry.

2. It is useful to have a boundaried space to work on, so use a piece of fabric, a cloth napkin or something similar opened out to create the 'stage' on which you will be working and that will contain the work.

3. Always start by asking the supervisee to pick something that stands for him or herself and to say a little about why that object was chosen and why he or she placed it where he or she did. This gives the supervisor some interesting insight about the supervisee. Then ask the supervisee to select and place an object that represents his or her client and say a little bit about that and its relationship to their object.

4. Ask him or her to add and place other figures in the 'picture' that are relevant to the case until he or she has finished describing the situation he or she has brought to the session. Try not to go back and forth too much from the supervisee as 'director of the scene' to supervisee in conversation about the scene back. Remember we are evoking the transpersonal so we want to stay with feeling quality present in the work. Analysis comes afterward when all has been said about the 'picture'.

5. It is important to stay in the world and language of the symbols and objects. As the picture unfolds ask questions framing them from within the story; for example, if the client has placed a rabbit to stand for his client, you could ask, "What does the rabbit see from here?" and "Who else can see the rabbit?" There is no judgment or direction of the figures by you, the supervisor.

6. When you have finished exploring things from all the perspectives within the story, only then ask questions like, "What may need to change here?" and "What would help this situation you have brought?"

7. When there are no more moves to be made and any connections, ideas and learning have been achieved from the experience the supervisor and supervisee can discuss it from how it was as an activity, what he or she took from it and any key phrases you may have captured to feed back. At this point you are back to your normal supervisor/supervisee conversation.

8. Ask the supervisee to return all the pieces to the basket and fold up the 'stage'. This contains the exercise and concludes it, too. Sometimes people like to take a picture of the first and last version of their work, especially if it has undergone quite a few changes, as a reminder.

## Final note

Do not touch the figures or the space of the picture because, for the duration of the piece of work, this is the *'temenos'* – the sacred space the supervisee is working in. The figures, however innocuous, become, during the activity, an extension of the supervisee's thinking, so respect says we do not touch them. This would apply equally to a drawing someone did. You can refer to it, of course, but don't handle it. This work honors the vital inner life of any individual where we are inviting and evoking. Never underestimate the power of the imagination. It can evoke moving and powerful responses.

# REFERENCES

## PRINT

**Bohm D (1980)** *Wholeness and the Implicate Order*, London, UK: Routledge.

**Buber M (1999)** *I and Thou*, London: Continuum Press.

**Silverstone, L (1997)** *Art Therapy the Person-centred Way: Art and the development of the person*, London, UK and Philadelphia, US: Jessica Kingsley.

**Vaughn, F (1986)** *The Inward Arc*, Boston, US and London, UK: Shambhala.

**Dogen, Ehei trans Tanahashi, Kazuaki (1986)** *Moon in a Dewdrop: Writings of Zen Master Dogen* North Point Press, New York

**Hookham, Shenpen (2006)** *Introduction to Formless Meditation*. The Shrimala Trust, Criccieth

**Ingram, Catherine (2003)** *Passionate Presence* Element, Portland Oregon

**Kabat-Zinn, Jon; Segal, Zindel V., Williams, J. Mark G.; Teasdale, John D.** (2006) *Mindfulness-based Cognitive Therapy for Depression: A New Approach to Preventing Relapse*. Guildford Press, New York & London

**Kabat-Zinn, Jon (2004)** *Wherever You Go, There You are: Mindfulness Meditation for Everyday Life* Piatkus, London

**Patterson, Elaine (2011)** in *Supervision in Coaching: Supervision, Ethics and Continuous Professional Development* ed. Jonathan Passmore; Kogan Page and Association for Coaching, London

Rodenburg, Patsy (2007),

**Presence, Penguin, London Senge Peter: Sharmer, C Otto; Jaworski, Joseph; Flowers, Betty Sue (2005),** *Presence* Nicholas Brearley, London & Boston

**Silsbee, Douglas (2008)** *Presence-Based Coaching*, Jossey-Bass, San Francisco

**Sogyal Rinpoche (1994)** *Meditation: A Little Book of Wisdom*. Harper Collins, San Francisco

**Thich Nhat Hanh (1999),** *Peace Is Every Step: The Path of Mindfulness in Everyday Life*. Rider, London

**Tolle, Eckhart (2005)** *A New Earth*, Penguin, London


## WEBSITES

**Barenboim (2006)** *Reith Lectures*, BBC archives, *www.bbc.co.uk*, [September 2010]


## FURTHER READING

**Briskin, A (1998)** *The Shelter of Soul in the Workplace*, San Francisco, US: Berrett-Koehler Publishers.

**Campbell, J (1976)** *The Hero with a Thousand Faces*, US: Princeton University Press.

**Edinger, E (1972)** *Ego and archetype*, , London and Boston: Shambhala.

**Hanson, Rick (2009)** *Buddha's Brain*, Oaklands, California, US: New Harbinger Publications.

**Hillman, J (1996)** *The Soul's Code*, London, UK: Bantam Book.

**Hollis, J (1993)** *The Middle Passage: From misery to meaning in midlife*, Toronto, Canada: Inner City Books.

**Hollis, J (2001)** *Creating a Path: Finding your individual path*, Toronto, Canada: Inner City Books.

**Jung, C (1953 revised 1968)** *Collected Works: The collective unconscious*, Vol. 9, London: Routledge, Kegan & Paul.

**Kornfeld, J (1993)** *A Path with Heart*, New York, US: Bantam Books.

**Moore, T (1992)** *Care of the Soul*, UK: Piatkus Press.

**Rowan, J (1993)** *The Transpersonal*, London, UK: Routledge.

Somers, B and Gordon-Brown, I (2002) *Journey in Depth*, ed. Hazel Marshall, Devon, UK: Archive Publishing.

**Thich Nhat Hahn (1975)** *The Miracle of Mindfulness*, London, : Rider.

**Welwood, J (1986)** *Wakening the Heart*, Boston,
US: Shambhala Press.

**Whyte. D (1994)** *The Heart Aroused*, London, UK: Industrial Society.

**Whyte, D (2002)** *Crossing the Unknown Sea*: *Work and the shaping of identity*, London, UK: Michael Joseph.

**Wilbur, Ken (1988)** *No boundaries*, Boston, US: Shambhala Press.

Wilbur, Ken ( )

**Wilde McCormick, E and Wellings, N (2000)** *Transpersonal psychotherapy theory & practice*, London, UK: Continuum.

**Zohar, D (1997)** *Rewiring the Corporate Brain*, San Francisco, US: Berrett-Koehler Publishers.

**Further Resources:**

## Coaching Supervision Academy

CSA is one of the pioneers in the development of supervision for coaches and a leading international provider of coaching supervision training and practical supervision support. The CSA Diploma in Coaching Supervision is accredited by EMCC and Approved by ICF. We have trained over 200 coach supervisors worldwide.

CSA also delivers Training in Supervision Skills to a wide range of professional and business groups and to internal coaches who wish to peer-supervise. We provide supervision to organizations, businesses and individual practitioners, worldwide.

**www.coachingsupervisionacademy.com**

## The Association of Coaching Supervisors

AOCS is an independent not-for-profit association formed by coach supervisors for coaches and supervisors.

Our mission is to:

▼ *Educate coaches and buyers about the vital work of supervision*

▼ *Raise the profile and promote the role of supervision worldwide*

▼ *Provide CPD and access to cutting edge articles, models, tools and supervision research*

**www.associationofcoachingsupervisors.com**


For further information on the Clean Language approach, see: Clean Language for Business: **www.cleancomm.co.uk** and  www.cleanlanguage.co.uk

For more information on TheoryU, see: **www.presencing.com**

Others who have influenced our work are:

Nancy Kline at **www.timetothink.com**

Dan Siegel at **www.drdansiegel.com**

# *Testimonials*

*"Supportive, generative, stretching and energising - regular supervision is simply essential for any coach who's serious about developing deep understanding, professionalism and effectiveness with their clients."*

**Linda Aspey,** President of AICTP (Assoc. of Integrative Coach-Therapist Professionals)

*"Supervision is essential for my coaching. It keeps me honest, grounded, in touch with my development goals – and I can talk about the work I love! "*

**Dr Henry Campion MB,BS.,**
Executive Coach and Coach Supervisor.

*"The ability to reflect carefully on one's work with an expert third party is crucial to maintaining coaching and mentoring standards. I see it as a professional duty to both clients and oneself."*

**Peter Neville Lewis,**
Founder - **Principled Consulting.** Director.
Board & SMT advice Ethical & Risk Culture & Strategy.